KNIT YOURSELF
Calm

KNIT YOURSELF

LYNNE ROWE
BETSAN CORKHILL

Calm

A creative path to managing stress

SEARCH PRESS

First published in 2017

Search Press Limited
Wellwood, North Farm Road,
Tunbridge Wells, Kent TN2 3DR

Photographs by Simon Pask

Cover photograph by Paul Bricknell at
Search Press Studios

ISBN: 978-1-78221-493-9

Suppliers

If you have difficulty in obtaining any of the materials and
equipment mentioned in this book, then please visit the
Search Press website for details of suppliers:
www.searchpress.com

You are invited to visit the authors' websites:
www.lynnerowe.weebly.com
www.stitchlinks.com

Printed in China by 1010 Printing International Ltd

Contents

Foreword by
Betsan Corkhill   8

Introduction   12

Materials & Tools   14

The Projects   18

Quick & Easy Projects   20

Washcloths   22
Unisex Scarf   24
Chunky Pillows   26

Portable Projects   28

Family Hats   30
    Technique: Knitting in
    the Round
Colour Block Cowl   34
Stripy Socks   36
    Techniques: Picking up
    Stitches and Kitchener Stitch

Group Projects   42

Patchwork Blanket   44
Bunting   48
Teddy Bear   52

Big Projects   56

Nursery Blanket   58

Shawl   62

Yarn Bag   66

New Skills Projects   70

Love Hearts Tea Cosy Set   72

    Technique: Fair Isle

Cabled Fingerless Mittens   78

    Technique: Cable Stitch

Evening Purse   86

Hot Water Bottle   90

    Technique: Duplicate Stitch

Essential Techniques   94

Tension (gauge)   96

Casting on   97

Casting off   99

Basic stitches   100

Increasing   102

Decreasing   103

Basic Stitch Patterns   104

Making a pompom   105

Blocking   106

Mattress Stitch   108

Abbreviations   110

Index   111

Acknowledgements   112

Foreword by Betsan Corkhill

Knitting is the perfect portable tool to enable you to manage the stresses and strains of everyday life, as well as those more challenging events that come everyone's way from time to time.

Jon Kabat-Zinn, who introduced 'mindfulness' to the Western world in the 1970s, believes in the importance of 'weaving your parachute' – acquiring the skills and knowledge you need when you are well so you already have them in place when life throws its inevitable challenges your way. In this book we will help you to 'knit your parachute' and discover the sanctuary of a calm, peaceful mind.

The idea of therapeutic knitting has been evolving gradually since 2005 when I began researching the meditative, creative and social benefits of knitting in relation to wellbeing. This work has shown that we can learn to use knitting as a tool to enhance its benefits in order to improve wellbeing and nurture a healthy brain.

Therapeutic knitting is the combination of knitting and knowledge; knowledge about your health and wellbeing, as well as about how you can use knitting to improve both. It can benefit us all and also be taken a step further to manage the symptoms of medical conditions.

Most of us will recognise the need to get back in control when life's major events come our way, but it is just as important to manage everyday stresses.

In fact, research has shown that the stress that builds up on an ongoing basis is more harmful to health than those bigger, life-changing events. Knitting combined with a knowledge about stress and its effects will enable you to stay in control.

A study I did with Cardiff University showed that the more frequently people knit (more than three times a week) the calmer and happier they feel – 81% felt happier after knitting. The same study showed that 54% felt happy or very happy, while fewer than 1% of those who were initially sad, remained sad. Excitingly, this finding translated to those with clinical depression.

The stress 'fight-or-flight' response evolved to protect us – to get us out of danger. It switches on systems that enable us to run or fight and switches off those not needed for immediate survival. Adrenaline and cortisol levels rise. The act of fighting or running away dissipates these chemicals and the body returns to its normal state.

This worked well for cavemen. However, the nature of modern-day stress is different. It takes the form of multiple ongoing stressors – looking after elderly parents, children, work-based issues, financial worries – which, although aren't directly life threatening, can become so if left unaddressed.

Stress can build up insidiously in the background to a point where you can forget what it feels like to be relaxed. This state of permanent 'alertness' can begin to feel normal for you. If this state persists over the longer term it will give rise to health problems. When your stress system is tuned up, your body's natural healing system – the rest and digest system – is tuned down.

Knitting provides you with a perfect tool to enable you to manage stress effectively, enjoyably and productively. It can also be used to address specific issues linked to stress to enable you to re-learn the feeling of relaxation, and even to rediscover more restful sleep.

Sleep can be severely disrupted during times of high stress because your brain stays alert to protect you. Knitting for 20 minutes or so before turning off the light can help you to switch off those thoughts for a better night's rest. If stress and worry wake you in the early hours, keep an easy project by your bedside to find calm.

The beauty of knitting is you can use it any time, anywhere, even on your commute to work or in your lunch break. If time is short, carry a project in your bag so you can knit yourself calm whenever you have a few spare minutes. Doing this regularly will make a difference – it will get your mind into the practice of 'being calm'. Your brain will learn that calm is a good place to be and you'll be able to recall this feeling at times when you don't have your knitting to hand.

A daily dose of knitting is great for managing stress. As you knit, focus on the calming, rhythmic movements and allow your mind to flow in harmony with your hands. Knitting on your own will enable you to focus on this feeling of calm, while knitting in a group will enhance your feelings of wellbeing. Raucous laughter is the hallmark of a knitting group so enjoy laughter and easy chat with your friends over coffee. It will tune down your stress fight-or-flight response.

You will soon find you can enter different mind states depending on the project you knit. A more complex one will distract your brain's attention from issues that may be detrimental to your wellbeing. An easy project can relax you into the rhythm of the process and encourage a state of daydreaming, giving your mind a complete break. Learning new skills will enable you to nurture a healthy brain to better manage stress. Why not give knitting mindfully a go? Focus on the texture of the yarn as it runs through your hands and contrast this with the firmness of the needles as your hands work rhythmically in the moment.

You will find a wide variety of projects in this book because variety is good for you. Each of the five sections has a specific purpose, so pick and choose your projects with thought about what you would like to achieve in terms of your wellbeing. I would recommend having a few on the go at the same time – perhaps one from each section? Think about how the texture and colours make you feel and choose your materials accordingly. The section on yarn and needles (see pages 14 and 15) will help you to do just this.

Learning to use knitting as a tool in this way will enhance its benefits, helping you to weave your life parachute and knit yourself calm.

Enjoy!

Introduction

Working with Betsan on *Knit Yourself Calm* has really changed my approach to knitting. As we chatted in person and exchanged emails, I began to learn more about the benefits of therapeutic knitting and how to apply it to my daily routine in order to help me manage the stresses and strains of everyday life. Not only do I now have a variety of works in progress to suit my mood and help me to switch off, meditate or relax, but I also have those I can turn to when I'm waiting for an appointment, taking a long journey or watching TV. These projects range from easy to more complicated designs, so I can either knit without needing to look at the pattern or, if the situation allows, I can sit and focus on something more complicated and demanding. I find that having a number of simple projects on the go at once is really productive, because I can pick something up and get knitting straight away, without wasting time trying to remember where I'm up to in the pattern, or which row comes next.

Having a busy and sometimes frantic lifestyle seems the norm for everyone these days, so it's even more important that at some point during the day we find a quiet moment of calm or somewhere to just sit, close our eyes, relax and shut out the world. Taking time out, even for 10 minutes, can really pick you up and help you feel refreshed. These stolen moments can often provide the perfect opportunity to knit and, with this in mind, I have designed 16 patterns to start you off on your therapeutic knitting journey. Used in conjunction with Betsan's ethos, these patterns will help you to make and meditate, and in the process you'll create some beautiful things for yourself and others. Projects include a pair of fingerless mittens that are perfect for autumn and spring, a cosy hot water bottle cover for wintry nights and a simple shawl. If you have a special evening out, the slipped stitch evening purse would make the perfect stylish accessory and a great opportunity to show off your knitting skills; or you could knit for the men in your life, all of whom would probably appreciate a pair of hand-knitted socks or a chunky scarf to keep them warm, knowing that every stitch has been woven with love. You can also knit for charity, creating a colourful patchwork blanket that you can work on with friends and donate to the charity of your choice.

Don't worry if you're new to knitting, as all the techniques and stitches you need are included within the projects themselves, or in the techniques section at the back of the book. If you make a start with the Quick & Easy Projects, you'll soon become familiar with the basics, and before you know it you'll be setting yourself new challenges, learning new skills and working in the round.

If you're a seasoned knitter, this book will become an essential tool for your therapeutic knitting journey. Creating something with your own hands can be meditative and rewarding, and ultimately something you can be proud of and cherish. Combining the therapeutic patterns with your favourite yarns and colours will ultimately bring you joy and satisfaction, so grab your favourite needles and yarn and knit your stresses away.

Happy knitting,

Lynne x

Materials & Tools

You don't need to go out and buy a huge amount of equipment to start knitting; the main essentials are a pair of needles and a ball of yarn.

The amount and wide range of knitting equipment on offer can be quite daunting, especially if you're new to knitting. The best way to start is to decide exactly what you want to knit and then buy the materials and equipment needed for that project. If you're a beginner, small and simple projects are a good way to start practising and improving your knitting skills, like those in Quick & Easy Projects, which are quick, fun and satisfying.

Each pattern in the book specifies the yarns needed, as well as needles and other items such as buttons and ribbons. You will also need some basic tools such as scissors, a wool needle and ruler. The following pages give a list of basic materials and tools that will be useful.

Yarns

The variety of yarns on the market is vast and hugely varied, so making a decision on which yarn to use can be overwhelming. You can buy anything from a thin lace-weight (1–3-ply) yarn through to a super chunky (super bulky) yarn that knits up quickly and creates a thick fabric.

As well as different weights, yarn is available in different types of fibre. Yarns can be natural, synthetic or a mixture of both. Synthetic yarns such as nylon, acrylic and polyester are all made from petro-chemicals. Rayon and viscose are made from the chemical treatment of cellulose fibres from wood pulp, and natural fibres are made from plant, animal and mineral sources. These include cashmere and mohair from goats, wool from sheep, alpaca from alpacas and angora from rabbits. Natural yarns are also derived from plants, such as cotton, bamboo, linen and hemp.

If you want to use a different yarn than recommended, then you need to match the tension (gauge) to the one given in the pattern. You will find all the information you need about a yarn on the ball band (the paper that is wrapped around a ball or skein of yarn). Check the yarn weight, fibre content and yardage and make sure it matches the yarn recommended. Knit up a swatch with your chosen yarn, following the instructions on page 96, to make sure you can achieve the correct tension (gauge) required. Each pattern in this book gives information about the type and weight of yarn used, so that you can use alternative yarn if desired.

Knitting needles

Basic knitting needles are not expensive and there is a wide variety available in both materials and types. You can also look out for second-hand needles in charity shops or thrift shops.

They come in different thicknesses to suit different yarn weights and there are three common sizing systems – metric (mm), old UK sizes and US sizes. The patterns in this book give the metric size first, followed by the old UK and US sizes in brackets. There is a conversion chart opposite to help you compare sizes.

You can buy regular straight needles, double-pointed needles (DPN), cable needles, circular needles, thick needles, thin needles – but the main point to remember is to buy the right needles for yourself and your project.

Knitting needles are made from plastic, wood, metal, bamboo or carbon fibre. While plastic, bamboo and carbon-fibre needles are lightweight, they can bend or warp and sometimes snap when working with tight stitches or cables. Ebony and Rosewood needles are sturdy and smooth with a more luxurious feel, but can be quite expensive. Aluminium needles tend to be cheaper, but they can be cold to the touch and problematic if you suffer with arthritis. You may need to experiment with a few different types of knitting needles before you find the ones that suit you most.

Straight needles: these are the traditional, classic needles that most people learn to knit with. With straight needles you can create flat pieces of fabric such as scarves or blankets. You cannot use them to create a seamless tube. They come in different lengths to suit different projects – short needles are perfect for small items, while longer needles are necessary for wider projects.

Circular needles and double-pointed needles (DPN): with these needles you can knit in the round to create a tube with no seam – perfect for the Portable Projects section (see page 28). Circular needles have two single-pointed needles at each end of a flexible cord, so you can knit in a circle and create a seamless fabric. You can also use long circular needles to knit in rows and create a piece of flat knitting – just turn after each row instead of working in the round. The Nursery Blanket (see page 58) in the Big Projects section uses this method.

Knitting in the round can also be achieved by using a set of 4 or 5 DPN, which are short needles pointed at both ends. These are used for projects that are too small for circular needles, such as small hats or socks.

Other essential items

Scissors

A pair of small, sharp scissors is a must for snipping yarn. If your scissors are sharp you may need to invest in a scissor case or sheath to cover the ends and avoid accidents. Don't be tempted to snap yarn with your hands as this can distort your knitting and will hurt your hands. If you need to line your projects, you will also need a pair of sharp fabric scissors.

Wool needle

A blunt-ended wool needle is useful when sewing up your work. Buy a needle with a large eye so that thicker yarn can be easily threaded and make sure it has a blunt end, as a pointed needle will split your yarn and spoil your knitting.

Ruler and tape measure

A see-through, hard ruler is essential when measuring your knitting tension (gauge) as it flattens the knitting nicely and gives an accurate measurement. A tape measure is also useful for measuring the length on longer pieces of work.

Metric Sizes	Old UK Sizes	US Sizes
2mm	14	0
2.25mm	13	1
2.75mm	12	2
3mm	11	–
3.25mm	10	3
3.5mm	–	4
3.75mm	9	5
4mm	8	6
4.5mm	7	7
5mm	6	8
5.5mm	5	9
6mm	4	10
6.5mm	3	10½
7mm	2	–
7.5mm	1	–
8mm	0	11
9mm	00	13
10mm	000	15
12mm	–	17
16mm	–	19
19mm	–	35
25mm	–	50

Rust-proof pins

These are vital for keeping things in place when sewing up your projects, for measuring out tension (gauge) squares and for blocking your work. Use pins with coloured heads so that they are visible and don't get lost in your knitting.

Stitch markers

These are round items like rings, usually made of plastic or metal. You can buy locking stitch markers that close like a safety pin or open stitch markers that can be removed or added at any time. You slip them onto your needles when instructed, to mark a place in your knitting, often where increases or decreases will take place, or where to start a pattern repeat. The Cabled Fingerless Mittens pattern on page 78 uses stitch markers.

Stitch holders

These can be really useful for holding stitches that are not in use. Stitches are slid to the stitch holders (without being knitted), then slid back to the needles when needed again.

Toy stuffing

Safety toy stuffing is recommended for children's toys, such as the Teddy Bear on page 52. Buy toy stuffing that states clearly whether it is safe, hygienic and washable. Polyester is a popular synthetic choice, but you can also buy organic or eco-friendly options that are biodegradable and less harmful to the environment.

Fabric pieces and ribbon

Some of the projects in this book are lined, so small amounts of fabric will be needed. Fabric can be bought in lengths (usually by the metre/yard) or you could use old clothes or bedding instead. Ribbon is also bought by the metre/yard and adds pretty and colourful dimension – perfect for hanging bunting (see page 48) or making bows on toys.

Bag handles

Some of the projects use bag handles, which can be bought from haberdashery shops or online shops and the size required is specified in the equipment list. If you prefer to knit your own bag handles, make sure you knit them in moss stitch or rib stitch. Lining them with fabric prevents stretching.

Purse frames

The Evening Purse on page 86 uses a purse frame. These can be glued in or sewn in, depending on your preference. If you use a glue-in frame, you will also need a glue gun.

Sewing needle and thread

These are useful for sewing lining fabric together (you can also use a sewing machine) and for sewing lining to your knitted fabric.

Pompom makers

These come in a range of sizes and are easy to use. You can also make pompoms by wrapping yarn around your hands or pieces of card (see Techniques, page 105).

Notebook and pen

These are a great alternative to a row counter and also useful for making notes as you knit and for jotting down any alterations or adaptations you decide to make to a pattern.

Other useful items

Ball-winder

Great for hanks or skeins of yarn that need to be wound into a ball before use, or for re-winding loose balls of yarn and leftovers. Yarn wound by a ball-winder is sometimes called a 'cake'.

Knitting needle size gauge

Some needles come without the size printed on the needle, so a needle size gauge is essential to find out the correct size of the needle. You simply poke your needles through the holes in a needle gauge to find out their size.

Row counter

This is handy to help you keep a note of how many rows you've knitted, but you need to remember to change the counter after completing each row. You can buy ones that sit at the base of a knitting needle, or ones that hang around your neck. You can even download row counter apps to your phone.

Project bag

The Yarn Bag on page 66 is a great place to keep your work in progress safe and clean.

The Projects

Quick & Easy Projects

I t's good to have more than one project on the go at any one time. Choose a
Quick & Easy one when you feel like a quick fix to raise your mood.
Use your favourite colours and textures to enhance the benefits of the
rhythmic movements and the feelgood effects. The feeling of success
you experience will motivate and inspire you.

Treat yourself to a colourful washcloth, keep warm with a snuggly scarf
or cuddle up to your very own handmade pillow. Look forward to and
focus on these cosy feelings as you knit.

Our Quick & Easy Projects make perfect presents too. The giving of gifts
has been shown to boost feelgood brain chemicals so as you knit, think about
those happy smiles when your lovingly made gifts are received.

Washcloths

These homely washcloths use very simple stitch patterns that are easy to remember. If you're new to knitting, they're a great way to practise new stitches and create something useful, while easing your mind into the flow of the movements.

To give as a gift, make one or two washcloths, fold each into a square, add a handmade soap and pop into a cellophane bag. Add a special message to a gift tag and tie around the top with matching yarn or ribbon.

Special Stitch instructions: Moss Stitch

Row 1: (K1, P1) to the last st, K1.

Rep row 1 as many times as stated.

Washcloths pattern

Moss Stitch Square

Using yarn A, cast on 45 sts.

Row 1: (K1, P1) to the last st, K1.

Row 1 forms the moss stitch pattern. Rep row 1 until your washcloth is square in shape. Cast off. Weave yarn ends into work and trim.

Broken Rib Square

Using yarn B, cast on 45 sts.

Row 1: K.

Row 2: (K1, P1) to the last st, K1.

Rows 1–2 form the pattern.

Rep rows 1–2 another thirty times (or until washcloth is a square shape).

Cast off. Weave yarn ends into work and trim.

Basketweave Square

Using yarn C, cast on 45 sts.

Row 1: K.

Row 2: (K5, P3) to last 5 sts, K5.

Row 3: (P5, K3) to the last 5 sts, P5.

Row 4: (K5, P3) to last 5 sts, K5.

Row 5: K.

Row 6: K1, P3, (K5, P3) to last st, K1.

Row 7: P1, (K3, P5) to last 4 sts, K3, P1.

Row 8: K1, P3, (K5, P3) to last st, K1.

Rows 1–8 form the pattern.

Rep rows 1–8 another six times, then rep rows 1–4 (60 rows in total). Cast off. Weave yarns ends into work and trim.

To finish

For all washcloths, steam block (see Techniques, page 107), pin flat and leave to dry completely.

Equipment

YARN

3 balls of aran (10-ply/worsted) yarn in orange (A), cream (B), and green (C); 50g/85m/92yd

KNITTING NEEDLES

4.5mm (UK 7, US 7) needles

TENSION (GAUGE)

Approx. 19 sts and 26 rows measure 10 x 10cm (4 x 4in) in st st, using 4.5mm (UK 7, US 7) needles. Tension (gauge) is not critical for this project

MEASUREMENTS

Approx. 23 x 23cm (9 x 9in)

Yarn notes

I used Rico Creative Cotton Aran, a 100% cotton yarn, which is available in a large range of colours. The colours I used are Fox (77), Natural (60) and Pistachio (41).

About the yarn

Unmercerised cotton such as Rico Creative Cotton Aran is the best type of yarn for this project as it absorbs water and can be washed over and over again. If you want to substitute yarn, any aran (10-ply/worsted) weight cotton will be suitable. Enjoy and explore a range of colour combinations.

Unisex Scarf

Get into the flow of this simple two-row pattern repeat to create this snuggly scarf. It will keep you warm when winter winds begin to bite. Knit it for family and friends to keep them cosy, too.

NOTE

If you want to make a wider or thinner scarf, you will need to add or subtract a multiple of 4 stitches plus 1 extra stitch.

Scarf pattern

Cast on 33 sts.

Row 1: K1, *P2, K2; rep from * to the end.

Row 2: P1, *K2, P2; rep from * to the end.

Rows 1 and 2 form a pattern called 'Mistake Rib', which is a variation on a standard rib pattern. The stitches are slightly offset and, unlike most ribs, it doesn't pull the fabric in. It is also reversible.

Rep rows 1 and 2 until you have approximately 1m (39½in) of yarn remaining. Cast off in pattern.

Making up

Weave all ends into WS and trim. If desired, spray block to loosen up the stitches (see Techniques, page 106) and stretch slightly when pinning flat. Leave to dry completely.

For a different finish, you could make two large pompoms and sew one to each end of the scarf (note: you will need an extra ball of yarn for the pompoms).

Equipment

YARN

3 balls of chunky (bulky) yarn in teal with flecks; 50g/90m/98yd

KNITTING NEEDLES

5mm (UK 6, US 8)

TENSION (GAUGE)

22 sts and 21 rows measure 10 x 10cm (4 x 4in) in 'Mistake Rib' pattern using 5mm (UK 6, US 8) needles

MEASUREMENTS

15 x 140cm (6 x 55in) unstretched

Yarn notes

I used King Cole Florence Chunky, an alpaca, wool and synthetic fibre blend (8% alpaca, 25% wool, 5% polyamide, 62% polyacrylic fibre). The colour I used is Everglade (2082).

About the yarn

This unisex scarf is made using King Cole Florence Chunky, which is a luxurious blend of wool, alpaca and polyamide. Richness of colour is created by twisting in a second colour, which produces a subtle self-patterning effect. It's beautifully soft and knits up quickly. You can substitute any standard chunky (bulky) weight yarn.

Chunky Pillows

Use the simplest of all stitches to give your mind a break from stress and strain. Choose colours that will brighten up your living room and mood. More calming tones will soothe you as you create these trendy home accessories.

Pillow pattern

Knit the pillow in one piece.

Using the yarn colour of your choice, cast on 33 sts.

Knit in garter stitch (every row knit) until your piece, when slightly stretched, fits around the pillow insert.

Cast off.

Making up

Fold the knitted piece in half with WS together and RS facing out. Sew the two sides of the pillow using mattress stitch (see Techniques, page 108) for a seamless finish, working through the bumps of the garter stitch row ends (working from the right side of the pillow). Weave yarn ends into WS and trim. Insert the pillow insert, then sew the remaining seam using mattress stitch. Tie off yarn ends and thread through to WS of pillow.

About the yarn

These cushions are knitted in Rowan Big Wool, a super-chunky (super bulky) yarn that is 100% wool. It's easy to knit with and gives great stitch definition as well as being soft and warm. It's available in a wide range of great colours so you can easily match it to your home décor. Any super chunky (super bulky) weight yarn with the same ball band tension (gauge) can be used.

Equipment

YARN

For 46cm (18in) square pillow:
3 balls of super chunky (super bulky) yarn in mink;
100g/80m/87yd

For 46 x 30cm (18 x 12in) rectangle pillow:
2 balls of super chunky (super bulky) yarn in ochre;
100g/80m/87yd

OTHER ITEMS

A 46cm (18in) square pillow insert or a 46 x 30cm (12 x 18in) rectangular pillow insert

KNITTING NEEDLES

12mm (no UK equivalent, US 17)

TENSION (GAUGE)

8 sts and 16 rows measure 10 x 10cm (4 x 4in) in garter stitch using 12mm (no UK equivalent, US 17) needles

MEASUREMENTS

To fit either a 46cm (18in) square pillow insert or a 46 x 30cm (18 x 12in) rectangular pillow insert

Yarn notes

I used Rowan Big Wool, a super chunky (super bulky) yarn that is 100% merino wool. The colours I used are Concrete (061) and Yoke (078).

Portable Projects

The smaller projects in this section are wonderfully portable, so keep one in your bag at all times. Use it to manage stress on the go, on your commute to work, in your lunch break, when travelling or at any other time when life is getting a bit much and you need to feel calm.

If you find yourself having to hang around in a waiting room, queue or traffic jam (as long as you're not driving!), use your portable project to turn your wait into a productive, calming experience. You may even find yourself wanting to wait longer.

Keep one by your bedside to calm your mind before sleep. Use it in the middle of the night if insomnia keeps you awake in the early hours. Its rhythm will soothe your soul.

Family Hats

These are perfect for the whole family – sizes are given for 0–6mths, 6–18mths, toddler to child, child to pre-teen, small adult and large adult. Use any DK (8-ply/light worsted) yarn and choose your family's favourite colours for a personal touch, or add a pompom for a bit of fun.

Worked in the round with simple decreases, these hats are a great portable project to use whenever you need to find calm while out and about. Read the step-by-step techniques section opposite on knitting in the round before you start.

NOTES

- The hats are knitted in the round on circular needles, so there is no seam to sew.
- When working stocking (stockinette) stitch in the round, every round is knit.
- Change to double-pointed needles during the decreasing rounds, when there are too few stitches to work comfortably on circular needles.
- If desired, for the largest 4 sizes (toddler to child/child to pre-teen/small adult/large adult), there is enough yarn to knit a deeper rib that can be folded in half.
- The large adult hat with a deep rib (not folded) also makes a great slouch beanie for a small-medium adult.

Hats pattern

Using 3.25mm (UK 10, US 3) circular needles, cast on 79(89/99/108/117/125) sts. Join in the round ready to start knitting, as follows (see also opposite):

Bring the tips of the needles together, making sure that the stitches are not twisted. Slip the top stitch from the right-hand needle to the left-hand needle and knit the top 2 stitches on the left-hand needle together as one stitch (78/88/98/108/116/124 sts).

Next, place your stitch marker on the right-hand needle to mark the start of the round and slip it on each round.

Equipment

YARN

1/1/2/2/2/2 balls of DK (8-ply/light worsted) yarn in blue, green or plum; 50g/112m/122yd

KNITTING NEEDLES

3.25mm (UK 10, US 3) circular needles (40cm length)

4mm (UK 8, US 6) circular needles (40cm length)

4mm (UK 8, US 6) DPN, set of 4 or 5

OTHER ITEMS

Stitch marker

TENSION (GAUGE)

Approx. 22 sts and 28 rows measure 10 x 10cm (4 x 4in) in st st, using 4mm (UK 8, US 6) needles

MEASUREMENTS

To fit 0–6mths/6–18mths/toddler to child/child to pre-teen/small adult/large adult

Finished circumference: 35/40/45/49/53/57cm (14/16/18/19½/21/22½in)

Finished depth: 12/14/17/19/20/21cm (5/5¾/6½/7½/8/8½in)

Yarn notes

I used Wendy Ramsdale DK yarn, which is 100% wool. The colours used are: Baby Hat – Blue (Bedale 3303), Pre-teen Hat – Green (Richmond 3308) and Adult Hat – Plum (Malton 3310).

Knitting in the Round

This is an alternative to using two straight needles and creates a knitted tube that has no seam to sew. You can use a long circular needle to knit a larger tube of knitting such as a sleeve or you can use a short circular needle for smaller items such as a hat or socks. Alternatively, you can use double-pointed needles (DPN) for these smaller items.

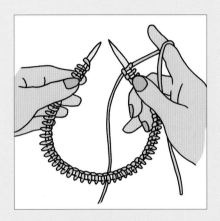

1 After casting on the required number of stitches, bring the tips of the needles together, making sure that the stitches are not twisted.

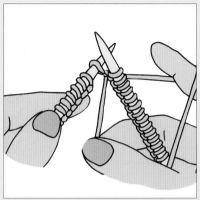

2 Slip the top stitch from the right-hand needle to the left-hand needle.

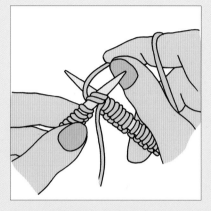

3 Knit the top 2 stitches on the left-hand needle together as one stitch. Your stitches are now joined and you are ready to work in the round.

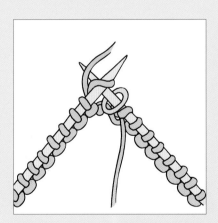

4 Place a stitch marker over the right needle to mark the start of the round, and slip it on each round.

Rib

Row 1: (K1, P1) to the end.

Rep row 1 until rib measures 2.5(3.75/3.75/3.75/4.5/4.5)cm (1/1½/1½/1½/1¾/1¾in) from cast on.

Note: There is enough yarn to knit a deeper rib that can be folded in half for sizes 45/49/53/57cm (18/19½/21/22½in). If desired for these sizes, rep row 1 until rib measures 7.5/7.5/9/9cm (3/3/3½/3½in).

For all sizes, change to 4mm (UK 8, US 6) circular needles.

Continue in st st until hat measures 7(7.5/10/10/12.5/12.5)cm (2¾/3/4/4/4½/5)in) from start of st st (top of rib section).

Decreasing

For 35/45/49/53/57cm (14/18/19½/21/22½in) sizes only:

[K11/47/25/27/29, K2tog) to the end (72/96/104/112/120sts).

For all sizes your stitch count is now divisible by 8 for the decrease rounds (72:88:96:104:112:120 sts).

Transfer stitches evenly between three or four DPN when the stitches are too few for your circular needles.

Round 1: (K6, K2tog) to the end (63/77/84/91/98/105 sts).
Round 2 and every alternate round: K.
Round 3: (K5, K2tog) to the end (54/66/72/78/84/90 sts).
Round 5: (K4, K2tog) to the end (45/55/60/65/70/75 sts).
Round 7: (K3, K2tog) to the end (36/44/48/52/56/60 sts).
Round 9: (K2, K2tog) to the end (27/33/36/39/42/45 sts).
Round 11: (K1, K2tog) to the end (18/22/24/26/28/30 sts).
Round 13: (K2tog) to the end (9/11/12/13/14/15 sts).

To finish

Cut yarn leaving a long tail end. Thread onto a wool needle and through the remaining sts, taking them off the knitting needle. Pull tight to gather the hole closed and fasten off yarn securely. Weave all loose yarn ends into the wrong side of work and trim. If desired, add a small- or medium-sized pompom to your hat.

About the yarn

These hats are made using Wendy Ramsdale DK, a 100% British Wool made from a blend of Masham fleece from the Yorkshire Dales. It is then dyed, spun and balled all in Yorkshire, UK. It is wonderful to handle, knits beautifully and comes in 12 gorgeous colours. If you want to substitute yarn, any DK (8-ply/light worsted) weight yarn is suitable.

Colour Block Cowl

Combine three of your favourite shades of yarn to create the striking colour-block effect in this cowl, or infinity scarf. Although the pattern is simple and repetitive, the result is contemporary and eye-catching and will give you a great sense of achievement.

Cowl pattern

Using yarn A, cast on 133 sts.

Join the stitches to start working in the round as follows (see also Family Hats, page 31):

Bring the tips of the needles together, making sure that the stitches are not twisted. Slip the first stitch from the right-hand needle to the left-hand needle and knit the first 2 stitches on the left-hand needle together as one stitch. You now have 132 sts.

Next, place your stitch marker on right-hand needle to mark the start of the round and slip it on each round.

Continue with Round 1:

Rounds 1–5: P for 5 rounds.

Rounds 6–15: K for 10 rounds.

Round 16–35: rep rounds 1–15 once more, then rep rounds 1–5.

Rounds 36–44: K for 9 rounds.

Change to yarn B. Cut yarn A.

Round 45: K.

Rounds 46–80: rep rounds 1–15 twice more then rep rounds 1–5.

Round 81: K.

Change to yarn C. Cut yarn B.

Rounds 82–90: K for 9 rounds.

Rounds 91–120: rep rounds 1–15 twice more.

Rounds 121–125: P for 5 rounds.

Cast off and weave yarn end through the first cast-off st to join the cast-off edge. Weave all ends into WS and trim.

To finish

Spray block (see Techniques, page 106), pin out to finished measurements and leave to dry completely.

Equipment

YARN

6 balls of DK (8-ply/light worsted) weight yarn: 2 balls each in petrol blue (A), light blue (B) and coral (C); 25g/55m/60yd

KNITTING NEEDLES

4mm (UK 8, US 6) circular needles 80cm (32in) in length

TENSION (GAUGE)

Approx. 22 sts and 30 rows measure 10 x 10cm (4 x 4in) in st st, using 4mm (UK 8, US 6) needles

MEASUREMENTS

When flat, approx. 30.5 x 39cm (12 x 15½in); circumference is approx. 61cm (24in)

Yarn notes

I used Erika Knight British Blue wool, a DK (8-ply/light worsted) pure wool yarn. The colours I used are petrol blue (Mr Bhasin 116), light blue (Iced Gem 108) and coral (Dance 112).

About the yarn

This striking colour block cowl is knitted in Erika Knight British Blue Wool, which is a DK (8-ply/light worsted) weight pure wool from the famous British breed Bluefaced Leicester sheep. It is grown, shorn, spun and balled in Britain (all within a 40-mile radius) and dyed using environmentally friendly dyes. British Blue is a soft yarn with great stitch definition and a slight sheen. Any standard DK (8-ply/light worsted) weight yarn can be substituted.

Stripy Socks

Wearing handmade socks is one of the most luxurious experiences your feet will have. They are incredibly warm and will remind you of the love that went into every stitch as you stride out into the world with cosy toes. Once you get used to the techniques involved – Picking up Stitches (page 38) and Kitchener Stitch (page 39) – you'll be knitting socks for everyone.

Socks pattern

Make 2.

Rib

Cast on 61(69/73) sts evenly onto four 3mm (UK 11, no US equivalent) DPN. Join to start knitting in the round as follows (see also Family Hats, page 31):

Bring the tips of the needles together, making sure that the stitches are not twisted. Slip the first stitch from the right-hand needle to the left-hand needle and knit the first 2 stitches on the left-hand needle together as one stitch. You now have 60(68/72) sts.

Next, place your stitch marker on right-hand needle to mark the start of the round and slip it on each round.

Round 1: (K2, P2) to the end.

Rep round 1 another sixteen times or until rib measures 4cm (1½in).

Leg

Work 47(57/61) rounds in st st (every row knit).

Heel

Row 1: K15(17/18), turn.

Row 2: P30(34/36), turn. Now work on these 30(34/36) sts only for the heel, working in rows using 2 DPN.

Row 3: (sl1, K1) to the end, turn.

Row 4: sl1, P to end, turn.

Rep rows 3 and 4 another fifteen times, or until heel measures 5cm (2in).

Equipment

YARN

100g of 4-ply (fingering) sock yarn in a variegated or solid shade; 100g/400m/437yd

KNITTING NEEDLES

Set of 5 3mm (UK 11, no US equivalent) DPN
Set of 5 2.5mm (UK 12, no US equivalent) DPN, or:
3mm (UK 11, no US equivalent) short circular needle
2.5mm (UK 12, no US equivalent) short circular needle or sizes needed to achieve correct tension (gauge)

OTHER ITEMS

3 stitch markers

TENSION (GAUGE)

32 sts and 44 rows to 10 x 10cm (4 x 4in) using st st in the round on 2.5mm (UK 12, no US equivalent) circular needles

MEASUREMENTS

Small/Medium/Large
S = approx. UK size 5–6 or 23cm (9in) length
M = approx. UK size 6–8 or 25cm (9¾in) length
L = approx. UK size 8–10½ or 27cm (10⅝in) length
Note: length of foot is adjustable to fit any shoe size.

Yarn notes

I used West Yorkshire Spinner's Signature 4-ply (fingering) yarn, which is 75% wool and 25% nylon. The colour I used is Passion Fruit Cooler (811).

Shape heel

Continue on the 30(34/36) heel sts:

Row 1: K17(19/20), skpo, K1, turn.

Row 2: sl1, P5, P2tog, P1, turn.

(Note: there is a gap between the stitches already knitted and the stitches waiting to be worked – use this as a marker for the following rows).

Row 3: sl1, K to 1 st before the gap, skpo, K1, turn.

Row 4: sl1, P to 1 st before the gap, P2tog, P1, turn.

Rep last 2 rows until all sts have been used up (18/20/20 sts).

(Note that on the last 2 rows for the largest size only, omit the K1 or P1 at the end of each row).

Technique

Picking up Stitches

If you're new to sock knitting then you may also be new to this essential technique. If you feel that it's a challenge, you could practise picking up stitches on a small square of knitting first, before starting your sock.

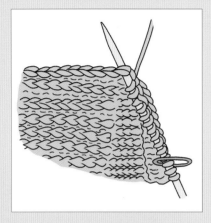

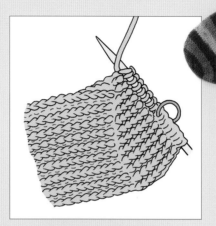

1 After completing the heel, find the first closest slipped stitch to the needle on your right. Insert DPN through **both** parts of the 'V' of the stitch, from front to back. Either use the same DPN or an empty DPN.

2 Wrap the working yarn around the DPN just like a knit stitch.

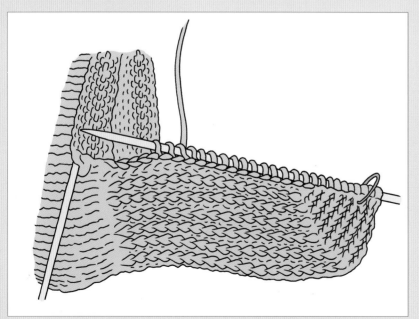

3 Bring the tip of the needle back through the slipped stitch to the front of your work, as if you are actually knitting it. You'll now have a new stitch on your working needle. This is called picking up and knitting. Continue this along the edge until you have picked up and knitted the correct number of stitches specified in the pattern, and make sure you work along a straight line for the neatest finish. If required, you can pick up an extra stitch between the gusset and the instep stitch in order to avoid any gaps in your socks. If you do this you will need to work an extra round (or two) of the gusset decreasing that follows.

Kitchener Stitch

Kitchener Stitch (or grafting) joins two sets of stitches that are still on needles (and haven't been cast off), by weaving a threaded wool needle through the stitches following the steps below. The result is invisible as it creates what looks like a knitted stitch between the two sets of stitches. This creates a really sturdy seam and can be used for shoulder seams on garments, as well as socks.

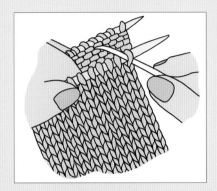

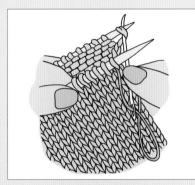

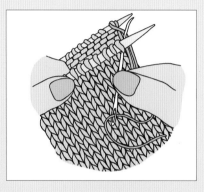

1 Hold the two sets of knitting needles parallel, with WS of knitting facing each other and RS facing outwards, with the tips of the needles pointing in the same direction. Thread yarn from the back piece onto a wool needle. Insert the wool needle into first stitch on front knitting needle as if to purl. Pull yarn through, leaving the stitch on the needle.

2 Insert the wool needle into the first stitch on the back needle as if to knit. Pull the yarn through, leaving the stitch on the needle.

3 Insert the needle into the first stitch on the front needle as if to knit and slip it off the end of the needle.

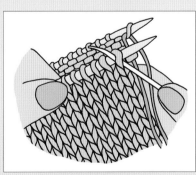

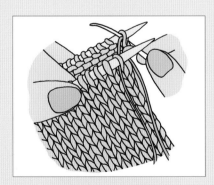

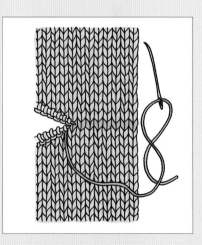

4 Insert the needle into the next stitch on the front needle as if to purl. Pull yarn through and this time leave the stitch on the needle.

5 Insert the needle into the first stitch on the back needle as if to purl, and slip it off the end of the needle.

6 Repeat steps 2–6 until the seam has been grafted together, stopping every so often to tighten up the stitches to create a tension (gauge) that matches your knitting.

Gusset

K across the 18(20/20) heel sts, pick up and knit 17 sts along the edge of the heel flap, 2 sts from gap between the end of the picked up sts and the next sts, K next 30(34/36) sts, pick up and knit 2 sts from gap before heel flap then pick up and knit 17 sts along the edge of the heel flap (86/92/94 sts). Place marker to mark the new start of the round (this stitch marker is not numbered).

Gusset shaping

Round 1: K34(36/36), K2tog, K1, place marker number 1, K30(34/36), place marker number 2, K1, skpo, K to end of round (84/90/92 sts).

Round 2: K all sts and slip all markers.

Round 3: K to 3 sts before marker 1, K2tog, K1, slip marker, K to next marker, slip marker, K1, skpo, K to end (82/88/90 sts).

Rep last 2 rounds until 60(68/72)sts remain, ending after round 3 and removing stitch markers 1 and 2 on last round. Keep the stitch marker in place that marks the start of the round.

Foot

Note: this part is adjustable and can be made long enough to fit any shoe size/foot length.

Continue in st st (every round knit) until sock measures approximately 18(20/22)cm (7/7¾/8¾in) from the back of the heel, or 5cm (2in) less than the desired finished length, ending last round at 6(7/8) sts before the marker (so leave last 6/7/8 sts unworked). Place marker, which indicates the start of the new round and continue with Toe.

Toe

Round 1: (K1, skpo, K24(28/30), K2tog, K1) twice, placing a second marker after first rep (56/64/68 sts).

Round 2: K all sts and slip markers.

Round 3: (K1, skpo, K to 3 sts before next marker, K2tog, K1) twice (52/60/64 sts).

Round 4: K all sts and slip markers.

Rep rounds 3 and 4 until 24(28/28) sts remain.

Divide sts over 2 DPN and use Kitchener stitch (see page 39) to graft toes together. Weave all ends into WS and trim.

Group Projects

Getting together with friends to knit, chat and laugh over coffee is one of life's joys. Supportive friends help us to live longer, healthier, happier lives so why not combine the calming nature of knitting with the support of being with friends? It's a powerful way to switch off your stress fight-or-flight response and switch on a bit of fun, play and laughter.

Planning group projects, working closely with others and being creative together will enhance the benefits. Why not knit our Patchword Blanket as a collective gift for a special person, or make it a group donation to charity? Celebrate life with colourful bunting that reflects your diverse personalities or make teddies together to give to children as special presents. It will make you feel good too.

Patchwork Blanket

Everyone in your knitting group can knit a square to contribute to this colourful joint project. Techniques range from simple stocking (stockinette) stitch to combining knit and purl stitches and playing with colour, ensuring that all abilities are catered for.

NOTE

 One 50g ball of Rico Creative Cotton Aran is enough to make two squares, so you could reduce the number of colours used and buy less yarn than specified. For the 25 squares you would need 13 balls of aran (10-ply/worsted) yarn (85m per ball), plus 2 extra balls for the border (15 balls in total).

Patchwork Blanket pattern

Square 1: Stocking (stockinette) Stitch

Make 9 (2 in purple, 2 in cream and 1 each in mustard, teal, burnt orange, fuchsia and pale green).

Using 4mm (UK 8, US 6) needles, cast on 35 sts.

Row 1 (RS): K.

Row 2: P.

Rows 1 and 2 form st st pattern. Rep rows 1 and 2 until 48 rows have been worked in total. Cast off, leaving a long tail end.

Square 2: Stocking (stockinette) Stitch Stripes

Make 4 (1 in light green and mid green; 1 in burnt orange and mid orange; 1 in teal and pale blue; and 1 in mustard and pale yellow).

Using 4mm (UK 8, US 6) needles and darker shade, cast on 35 sts.

Row 1 (RS): K.

Row 2: P.

Change to lighter shade and continue in st st, in stripes of 2 rows of lighter shade/2 rows of darker shade, until 46 rows have been worked in total (ending after 2 rows of darker shade).

Next row: K in darker shade. Cast off, leaving a long tail end of yarn.

Square 3: Garter Stitch Lines

Make 6 (1 in each in grey, fuchsia, pale blue, pale yellow, cream and mid green).

Using 4mm (UK 8, US 6) needles, cast on 37 sts.

Row 1 (WS): P.

Row 2: K.

Equipment

YARN

19 balls of aran (10-ply/worsted) yarn in 12 different colours: 3 in teal, 2 each in mustard, purple, cream, grey and pale blue; 1 each in pale green, mid green, pale yellow, burnt orange, mid orange and fuchsia; 50g/85m/92yd

KNITTING NEEDLES

3.75mm (UK 9, US 5)
4mm (UK 8, US 6)
4mm (UK 8, US 6) circular needles (80 or 100cm (32 or 39in) length) for working the border (in rows)

TENSION (GAUGE)

Using needle size specified, each square should measure approx. 18 x 18cm (7¼ x 7¼in). Tension (gauge) is not critical for this project, but try to make sure that each square measures the same size throughout.

MEASUREMENTS

Finished blanket measures approx. 92 x 92cm (36¼ x 36¼in)

Yarn notes

I used Rico Creative Cotton Aran, which is 100% cotton. The colours I used are Petrol (47), Mustard (70), Cardinal (11), Natural (60), Pearl Grey (52), Smokey Blue (31), Light Pistachio (44), Pistachio (41), Vanilla (62), Fox (77), Smokey Orange (72) and Fuchsia (13).

About the yarn

The blanket is made using Rico Creative Cotton Aran, which is available in a large range of colours and is great value for money. Choose from bright jewel shades or muted pastels to create your own colour combinations. It is perfect for summer blankets and is machine washable too. If you want to substitute yarn, any aran (10-ply/worsted) weight yarn is suitable. You can also use a different weight yarn for your blanket, but your square will turn out either smaller (with a lighter weight yarn) or bigger (with a heavier weight yarn).

Rows 3–8: rep rows 1 and 2 another three times.

Row 9: K.

Rows 10–16: beginning with a K row, work 7 rows in st st.

Row 17: K.

Rep rows 10–17 another three times.

Rows 42–49: beginning with a K row, work 8 rows in st st.

Cast off, leaving a long tail end.

Square 4: Basketweave

Make 2 (1 in pale blue and 1 in grey)

Using 4mm (UK 8, US 6) needles, cast on 37 sts.

Row 1 (RS): K.

Row 2: (K5, P3) to last 5 sts, K5.

Row 3: (P5, K3) to the last 5 sts, P5.

Row 4: (K5, P3) to last 5 sts, K5.

Row 5: K.

Row 6: K1, P3, (K5, P3) to last st, K1.

Row 7: P1, (K3, P5) to last 4 sts, K3, P1.

Row 8: K1, P3, (K5, P3) to last st, K1.

Rows 1–8 form the pattern. Rep rows 1–8 another five times, then rep rows 1–4 (52 rows in total).

Cast off leaving a long tail end of yarn.

Square 5: Dot Stitch

Make 4 (1 each in mustard, cream, grey and purple).

Using 3.75mm (UK 9, US 5) needles, cast on 39 sts.

Row 1 (RS): K.

Row 2: (P3, K1) to last 3 sts, P3.

Row 3: K.

Row 4: P.

Row 5: K.

Row 6: P1, K1, (P3, K1) to last st, P1.

Row 7: K.

Row 8: P.

Rows 1–8 form the pattern. Rep rows 1–8 another five times then rep rows 1–3.

Cast off leaving a long tail end.

To finish

Place squares into a grid of 5 x 5 squares, in your preferred order. Sew squares using tail ends of yarn and use mattress stitch (see page 108) for a really neat finish. Weave in all yarn ends to WS and trim.

Border

With RS of blanket facing, use circular needles to pick up and knit 165 sts along one edge.

Row 1 (WS): (K1, P1) to the last st, K1.

Row 2: rep row 1.

Row 3: Kfb, (P1, K1) to the last 2 sts, P1, Kfb (167 sts).

Row 4: Pfb, (K1, P1) to the last 2 sts, K1, Pfb (169 sts).

Rep rows 3 and 4 twice more then rep row 3 (179 sts).

Cast off.

Rep all border instructions for each of the remaining sides.

To finish

Sew the mitred corners together. Weave ends into WS and trim. Steam block using an iron and a cloth (see Techniques, page 107). Do not place the iron directly onto the cotton fabric. Lay flat and leave to dry.

Bunting

Bunting makes people smile. Customise yours to create a unique visual statement such as 'Just Married', 'Happy Birthday' or 'Congratulations'. Coordinate colours, add pompoms and allow your creative mind to run free. Make it together with friends to add another dimension to the benefits this project will bring.

Bunting pattern

Top border

Using yarn A, cast on 23 sts (starting at the ribbon channel).

Rows 1–5: starting with a K row, work 5 rows in st st.

Row 6 (fold line): K.

Rows 7–10: starting with a K row, work 4 rows in st st. Continue with main pennant.

Main pennant

Rows 1 and 2: K.

Row 3: K1, skpo, K to last 3 sts, K2tog, K1 (21 sts).

Row 4: K.

Rows 5–36: rep rows 1–4 eight times (5 sts).

Rows 37–38: K.

Row 39: skpo, K1, K2tog (3 sts).

Rows 40–42: K.

Row 43: K1, K2tog, pass first st on right needle over the second to cast off. Cut yarn, leaving a long tail end and fasten off.

Fold ribbon channel in half to the WS and pin in place. Slip stitch the cast-on edge to the main pennant using tail end of yarn.

Make two more pennants in yarn A, two in yarn B and two in yarn C.

Equipment

YARN

3 balls of aran (10-ply/worsted) yarn in pale pink (A), red (B) and fuchsia (C); 50g/75m/82yd

KNITTING NEEDLES

4mm (UK 8, US 6) needles

OTHER ITEMS

1.5m (1¾yd) length of ribbon, 1.5–2cm (¾in) wide
Scraps of contrast fabric
Small piece of medium weight iron-on fabric backing
22cm (9in) felt square in deep pink for letters (or use die-cut felt letters)
PVA glue or double-sided tape

TENSION (GAUGE)

Approx. 19 sts and 38 rows measure 10 x 10cm (4 x 4in) in garter stitch, using 4mm (UK 8, US 6) needles; tension (gauge) is not critical for this project

MEASUREMENTS

Each pennant measures approx. 12 x 13.5cm (4¾ x 5½in)

Yarn notes

I used DMC Natura Medium, a 100% cotton yarn. The colours I used are Pale Pink (04), Red (05) and Deep Pink (444). One ball makes three pennants.

Fabric embellishments

Iron the fabric backing onto the WS of your fabric. Use a pencil to draw six circles approximately 5cm (2in) across. Carefully cut out the circles. The fabric backing will stop the fabric from fraying. Spread PVA glue onto the WS of each fabric circle (onto the fabric backing). Place each circle onto the centre front of each pennant and press gently into place and leave to dry.

Adding felt letters

If you have purchased die-cut felt letters, use PVA glue or double-sided tape to stick each letter to the centre of each fabric circle. If you make your own letters, cut these from felt, approximately 3cm (1¼in) long then stick to each fabric circle.

To finish

Thread the ribbon through each pennant and hang your bunting.

Variations

Add buttons instead of letters and attach a pompom (see Techniques, page 105) to the point of each pennant.

About the yarn

This strip of bunting is made using DMC Natura Medium, a 100% cotton yarn, which is available in a bright rainbow of colours. Cotton is great yarn for bunting as it is slightly heavier than other types, so when it is combined with garter stitch the edges stay nice and flat. If you want to substitute yarn, any aran (10-ply/worsted) weight yarn is suitable.

Teddy Bear

Make and give teddies as a group to improve someone else's life. This simple teddy bear is the perfect project for using up all those oddments in your yarn stash, as well as making something cute for someone who may need a cuddle.

> **NOTE**
>
> Each leg is knitted first then joined together for the body and head. There is no increasing or decreasing, so this teddy bear is great for beginners.

Teddy Bear pattern

Leg 1

Using yarn A, cast on 18 sts.

Row 1 (WS): K.

Rows 2–33: K every row.

Cut yarn. Slide sts to bottom of needle and leave them there while you knit the second leg.

Leg 2

Cast on 18 sts onto your free needle.

Rep all instructions as given for Leg 1 but do not cut yarn after row 33.

Body

Row 1 (RS): K across sts of Leg 2 then K across sts of Leg 1 (36 sts).

Row 2 (WS): K.

Next, work 32 rows in g st (knit every row). Mark the ends of the last row with small pieces of waste yarn, then continue with the head.

Equipment

YARN

1 ball of DK (8-ply/light worsted) yarn in pale blue or yellow (A) Oddments of DK (8-ply/light worsted) yarn in red for neck tie (B) and black for face (C); 50g/113m/124yd

KNITTING NEEDLES

3.5mm (no UK equivalent, US 4)

OTHER ITEMS

Toy stuffing

TENSION (GAUGE)

Not critical

MEASUREMENTS

Approx. 21.5cm (8½in) long

Yarn notes

I used Rooster Almerino DK, which is 50% baby alpaca and 50% merino. The colours I used are Custard (210) and Beach (217). One ball makes one teddy bear.

About the yarn

Rooster Almerino DK is really soft, has a tight twist and gives beautiful stitch definition. The colour range is varied and well co-ordinated, so all the colours look great on their own, or when combined. Any weight yarn can be used as a substitute, together with needles that are the next size smaller than recommended on the yarn band. If you use a lighter weight yarn your teddy will turn out smaller and if you use a heavier weight yarn your teddy will turn out larger.

Head

Work 28 rows in g st.

Cast off. Cut yarn leaving a long 45cm (18in) tail end.

Arms (make 2)

Using yarn A, cast on 15 sts.

Row 1 (WS): K.

Rows 2–25: K every row.

Cast off.

Make second arm following all instructions above.

Sewing up

Note: when sewing seams together, use mattress stitch and work from the RS – working through the garter stitch bumps at the ends of the rows.

Place the head/body piece flat with WS uppermost and the head at the top. Fold the sides in towards the centre and stitch the centre back body seam from the top down to the legs, using whip stitch or mattress stitch with matching yarn and working from the RS of work. Do not cut yarn.

Next, stitch the inside leg seams with matching yarn, using mattress stitch or whip stitch. Do not cut yarns.

Use yarn ends to close any gaps that may exist where the back seam joins the leg seams.

The feet and head seams remain open. Push toy stuffing through the open seams to fill the head, body and legs, keeping the teddy more flat-shaped, rather than rounded. Next, stitch the top head and foot seams using whip stitch with matching yarn.

Fold arms in half and whip stitch around cast-on edge and side seams. Fill lightly with toy stuffing then stitch open edge of arms to sides of body.

Thread a length of yarn A onto a wool needle and stitch small running stitches all around the marked row, starting from the centre back. Pull yarn gently to create a neck and tie yarn. Weave ends into body.

Neck tie

Using yarn B, make a twisted cord, following instructions below (or you could use a length of ribbon).

Twisted cord

Take a length of yarn 3m (3¼yd) long. Fold the yarn in half and place the folded loop around a door handle, or pin it securely to a pillow. Knot the two yarn ends together and place a pencil in this loop. Pull the yarn tight and rotate the pencil so that the yarn begins to twist. Keep going until the twists are really tight and the cord starts to kink when the pencil is relaxed.

Lift the yarn off the door handle or pillow carefully, so that it doesn't unwind. Fold the cord in half, letting it twist around itself to make a thicker cord and knot the two ends together.

To finish

Using yarn A, make a small stitch through each top corner of the head, to create ears. Using yarn C, stitch two eyes and a 'T' for the nose, using the photographs as guidance.

Place the cord around the teddy's neck and tie in a bow. If necessary, knot the ends of the cord nearer to the bow and trim the ends below the knots. For extra safety, stitch in place firmly to the neck with sewing thread at the back of the neck and also through the bow at the front of the neck.

Big Projects

It's a lovely cosy feeling to sit quietly at home with your Big Project on your lap, keeping you warm as you knit. Let it be your constant friend, the one you turn to to find calm and consistency when the world around you feels a bit frantic. As you get into the flow of the pattern, its familiarity will enable you to settle into a soothing rhythm whenever you need to knit yourself calm.

Don't give yourself a deadline to finish your Big Project. Simply allow the process to take you at the speed you need to go in the moment. Focus solely on this process as your hands work rhythmically, allowing your mind and thoughts to flow as you go. Return to it whenever you need to. It will be there for you.

Nursery Blanket

A new arrival in the world is an exciting event. This cosy, super-soft blanket uses a simple two-row pattern in contrasting colours to create a stunning chevron design. Make it as a special gift to celebrate a new beginning. It will keep baby snug and make you smile, too.

NOTE

 Circular needles are used to work the blanket in rows because regular knitting needles are too short for the number of stitches used.

Nursery Blanket pattern

Using yarn A, cast on 118 sts.

Row 1: K5, (Kfb, K6, skpo, K2tog, K6, Kfb) six times, K5.

Row 2: K.

Rows 3–6: rep rows 1 and 2 twice more.

Row 7: rep row 1.

Row 8: K5, P to last 5 sts, K5.

Rows 9–20: rep rows 7 and 8 another six times.

Change to yarn B.

Rows 21–40: rep rows 7 and 8 ten times.

Change to yarn A.

Rows 41–54: rep rows 7 and 8 seven times.

Change to yarn C.

Equipment

YARN

3 balls of aran (10-ply/worsted) yarn in cream (A), 1 ball each in mustard (B), coral (C) and blue (D); 50g/115m/126yd

KNITTING NEEDLES

5mm (UK 6, US 8) circular needle (100cm (39in) length)

TENSION (GAUGE)

1 pattern repeat of B, C or D (20 rows) using 5mm (UK 6, US 8) needles measures approx. 8.5cm wide x 7.75cm deep (3½in wide x 3in deep)

MEASUREMENTS

Approx. 54 x 76cm (21¼ x 30in) after blocking

Yarn notes

I used Sublime Evie, a mix of 94% cotton and 6% nylon yarn. The colours I used are Nougat (508), Ochre (513), Zola (515) and Luna (516).

About the yarn

The yarn for this gorgeous baby blanket, knitted in Sublime Evie, is made in Italy and contains the finest Mako cotton. It is a lightweight yarn and perfect for both summer and winter knitting. The yarn is slightly coarse in texture but creates a beautifully soft fabric with plenty of drape. The colour range is stunning and the whole palette works well together, or individually. The yarn can be handwashed or dry cleaned. Substitute any aran (10-ply/worsted) weight yarn of a similar yardage and use 5mm (UK 6, US 8) knitting needles.

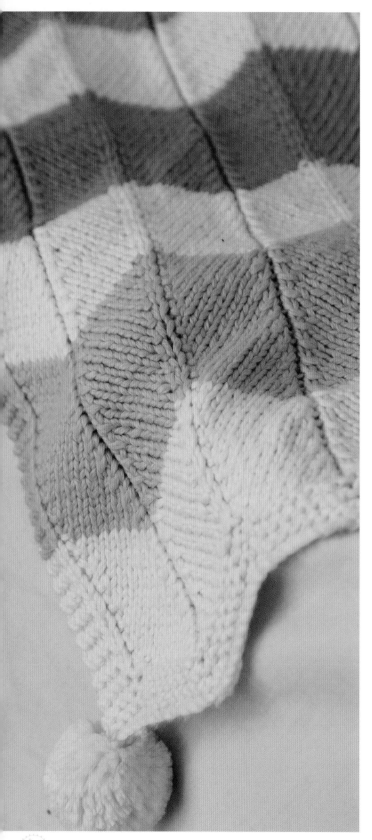

Rows 55–74: rep rows 7 and 8 ten times.

Change to yarn A.

Rows 75–88: rep rows 7 and 8 seven times.

Change to yarn D.

Rows 89–108: rep rows 7 and 8 ten times.

Change to yarn A.

Rows 109–122: rep rows 7 and 8 seven times.

Change to yarn C.

Rows 123–142: rep rows 7 and 8 ten times.

Change to yarn A.

Rows 143–156: rep rows 7 and 8 seven times.

Change to yarn B.

Rows 157–176: rep rows 7 and 8 ten times.

Change to yarn A.

Rows 177–190: rep rows 7 and 8 seven times.

Rows 191–196: rep rows 1 and 2 three times.

Cast off, maintaining row 1 pattern as follows:

Cast off first 4 sts (1 st now on right needle), *Kfb (3 sts on right needle), slip first st on right needle back to left needle (2 sts now on right needle), lift the second stitch on right needle over first st to cast off, slip first st on left needle back to right needle, lift the second stitch on right needle over first st to cast off (1 st on right needle), cast off next 6 sts (1 st on right needle), skpo, (2 sts now on right needle), lift the second stitch on right needle over first st to cast off, K2tog, lift the second stitch on right needle over first st to cast off, cast off next 6 sts, Kfb (3 sts on right needle), slip first st on right needle back to left needle (2 sts now on right needle), lift the second stitch on right needle over first st to cast off, slip first st on left needle back to right needle, lift the second stitch on right needle over first st to cast off (1 st on right needle); rep from * another five times, cast off remaining sts.

To finish

Weave all ends into WS and trim. Spray with cold water and pin flat to finished dimensions above. Leave to dry completely. Add small pompoms (see Techniques, page 105) to each corner of the blanket.

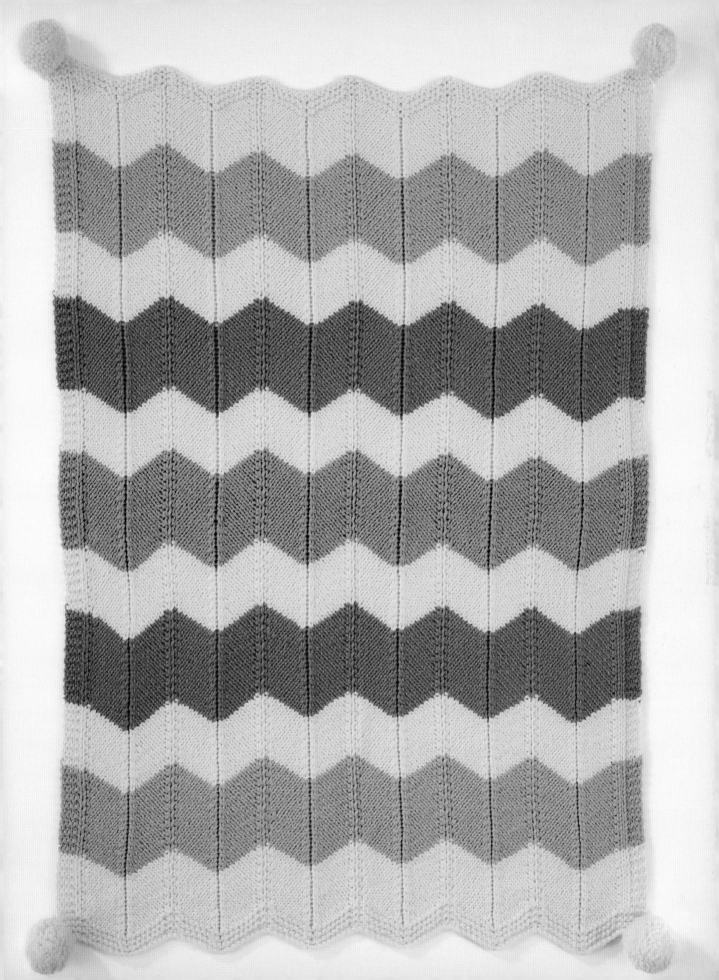

Shawl

Even if you are new to knitting, the easy pattern in this shawl will soon become familiar. The lace section is very simple and the picot cast-off is repetitive and easy to memorise. Go with the flow, trust in the pattern and enjoy creating your very own statement wardrobe accessory.

Equipment

YARN

4 balls of DK (8-ply/light worsted) yarn: 2 in blue (A) and 1 in each in grey (B) and red (C); 50g/100m/110yd

NEEDLES

4.5mm (UK 7, US 7) circular needles (80 or 100cm (32 or 39in) length) (to knit in rows)

OTHER ITEMS

Stitch marker

TENSION (GAUGE)

Approx. 18 sts and 28 rows measure 10 x 10cm (4 x 4in) in st st, using 4.5mm (UK 7, US 7) needles (after blocking)

MEASUREMENTS

After blocking, 120cm wide and 49.5cm deep (47¼ x 19½in)

Yarn notes

I used King Cole Baby Alpaca DK, a 100% baby alpaca yarn. The colours I used are Evergreen (665), Grey (502) and Cranberry (510).

Note

 Circular needles are used to work the shawl in rows because regular knitting needles are too short for the number of stitches used.

Shawl pattern

Using yarn A, cast on 5 sts.

Row 1: K1, Kfb, K1, Kfb, K1 (7 sts).

Row 2: K2, Kfb, K1, Kfb, K2 (9 sts).

Place a stitch maker in the centre stitch (this is the 5th stitch along) and move it up every few rows so that you can easily see the stitch. This marks the centre stitch and avoids the necessity of counting.

Garter stitch section

Row 3: K2, Kfb, K up to the centre st, yrn, K1 (this is the centre st), yrn, K to last 3 sts, Kfb, K2 (13 sts).

Row 4: K2, Kfb, K to the last 3 sts, Kfb, K2 (15 sts).

Rows 5–18: rep rows 3 and 4 another seven times (57 sts).

Stocking (stockinette) stitch section

Row 19: K2, Kfb, K up to the centre st, yrn, K1 (this is the centre st), yrn, K to last 3 sts, Kfb, K2 (61 sts).

Row 20: K2, Kfb, P to 1 stitch before the centre st, K3 (these are the centre stitch and the 2 yrn sts on either side), P to the last 3 sts, Kfb, K2 (63 sts).

Rep rows 19 and 20 another eleven times (129 sts).

Garter stitch section

Rep rows 3 and 4 another eight times (177 sts).

About the yarn

This beautiful shawl is knitted in King Cole Baby Alpaca, made from the first cut of the baby alpaca's coat. It creates a soft and luxurious fabric that is hard wearing, light and warm, which is perfect for accessories and garments. It knits up to a standard double knitting weight, so any DK (8-ply/light worsted) yarn can be substituted. The yarn is handwash only.

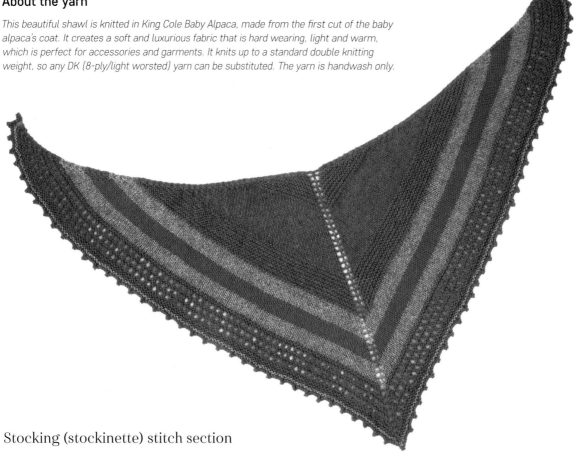

Stocking (stockinette) stitch section

Rep rows 19 and 20 another twelve times in the following colour sequence (cutting yarns after each 8 rows of colour):

8 rows yarn B; 8 rows yarn C; 8 rows yarn B (249 sts).

Lace section

Use yarn A.

Next row: K2, Kfb, K up to the centre st, yrn, K1 (this is the centre st), yrn, K to last 3 sts, Kfb, K2 (253 sts).

Next row: K2, Kfb, K to the last 3 sts, Kfb, K2 (255 sts).

Rep last 2 rows once more (261 sts).

Next row: K2, Kfb, (K2tog, yrn) to 2 sts before the centre st, K2, yrn, K1, yrn, K2, (yrn, K2tog) to the last 3 sts, Kfb, K2 (265 sts).

Next row: K2, Kfb, K to the last 3 sts, Kfb, K2 (267 sts).

Next row: K2, Kfb, K up to the centre st, yrn, K1 (this is the centre st), yrn, K to last 3 sts, Kfb, K2 (271 sts).

Next row: K2, Kfb, K to the last 3 sts, Kfb, K2 (273 sts).

Rep last 4 rows twice more (297 sts).

Garter stitch section

Rep rows 3 and 4 another three times in the following colour sequence: 2 rows yarn C; 2 rows yarn B; 2 rows yarn C (315 sts).

Cast off

Cast off 3 sts, *pass the st on the right needle back to the left needle, cast on 2 sts using a 2-needle cast-on method, cast off 6 sts; rep from * until all sts are cast off. Cut yarn and pull through last st on needle.

To finish

Wet block (see Techniques, page 107) and pin out to measurements given at beginning of pattern. Leave to dry completely.

Yarn Bag

Simple stripes of different stitches are used here to create a useful holdall for your knitting. Add leather handles to create a professional finish and a very stylish bag. Feel pride in yourself as you carry it around.

Special Stitch instructions: Moss Stitch

Row 1: (K1, P1) to the last st, K1.

Rep row 1 as many times as stated.

Stripy Bag pattern

Front and back (make 2)

Using 4.5mm (UK 7, US 7) needles and yarn A, cast on 73 sts.

Work in moss stitch until work measures 7.5cm (3in) from cast-on edge, ending with RS facing.

Change to yarn B.

Beginning with a K row, work in st st for 5cm (2in), ending with RS facing.

Change to yarn C.

K one row then work in moss stitch for 5cm (2in), ending with RS facing.

Change to yarn B.

Beginning with a K row, work in st st for 5cm (2in), ending with RS facing.

Change to yarn A.

K one row then work in moss stitch for 5cm (2in), ending with RS facing.

Change to yarn B.

Beginning with a K row, work in st st for 5cm (2in), ending with RS facing.

Change to 4mm (UK 8, US 6) needles for top edge of bag and work top section in 2 colours (yarn A and yarn C).

Carry unused yarn across back of work when not in use.

Cut yarn B.

Equipment

YARN

3 balls of aran (10-ply/worsted) yarn: 1 ball each of red (A), cream (B) and grey (C); 100g/200m/219yd

NEEDLES

4mm (UK 8, US 6) 4.5mm (UK 7, US 7)

OTHER ITEMS

0.5m (½yd) contrast fabric Sewing needle and thread Set of two sew-on black leather bag handles, 71cm (28in) long

TENSION (GAUGE)

Approx. 21 sts and 28 rows measure 10 x 10cm (4 x 4in) in stocking (stockinette) stitch, using 4.5mm (UK 7, US 7) needles; tension (gauge) is not critical for this project

MEASUREMENTS

After blocking, approx. 34cm wide and 38cm deep (13½ x 15in)

Yarn notes

I used Rowan Pure Wool Worsted yarn, which is 100% wool. The colours I used are Rich Red (124), Cream (102) and Granite (111).

Note

 When changing colour, leave long tail ends (approx. 20cm/8in) of yarn for sewing seams at the end.

Top edge

Row 1: (K1 in yarn A, K2 in yarn C) to last st, K1 in yarn A.

Row 2: (P1 in yarn A, P2 in yarn C) to last st, P1 in yarn A.

Rep rows 1 and 2 for 5cm (2in) in total, ending with RS facing.

Cut yarn A.

K one row in yarn C.

Next row (top fold line): K.

Continue in yarn C for inside hem.

Beg with a K row, work 14 rows in st st.

Cast off.

To finish

Spray block both pieces to the same size (see Techniques, page 106). Leave to dry completely.

   Place front and back pieces together with WS together and RS outermost. Join side and bottom seams using mattress stitch (see page 108) and matching yarn. Mattress stitch creates a neater and less bulky seam. Tie off and trim all yarn ends inside the bag.

   Using bag as a template (with top hem folded to inside), cut out two pieces of fabric, adding 1cm (½in) extra all round for seam allowance. Stitch sides and bottom of fabric pieces with RS together. Turn top edge seam allowance of lining to WS and stitch in place.

   Slide lining into bag with WS of lining against WS of bag. Slip stitch lining to bag round fold line of hem. Place straps in place on each side of bag and stitch to bag through lining for stability. Fold knitted hem of bag to inside and slip stitch to lining.

New Skills Projects

Learning new skills on a regular basis is essential for nurturing a healthy brain, opening new neural pathways and even encouraging the growth of new brain cells right into old age. This section focuses on a range of new skills to encourage you to experiment with different stitch patterns and combinations of colour and textures. They are designed specifically to stimulate your creative mind.

Thinking creatively is important for wellbeing and is a skill that is transferable to all areas of life. It opens up more options to you when life throws its challenges your way.

When you've mastered these skills, experiment by using them in other projects with different colour combinations so that you keep learning and knitting a healthy, flexible, calm mind throughout your life.

Love Hearts Tea Cosy Set

Fair Isle knitting can create bold, visual patterns. These small projects are a great introduction to the art of Fair Isle and an effective way of practising this new skill before moving on to a larger project. Take a look at the technique information below and opposite before you start.

Fair Isle knitting notes

For Fair Isle, a chart is usually provided in the form of a grid with each square representing one stitch. Each square on the grid is coloured to show the yarn to be used for each stitch. It helps to keep the two balls of yarn separate while knitting, in order to prevent them from tangling. Keep one ball on your right and one ball on your left.

As you change colours, simply let the old colour hang down at the back of the work until needed again and pick up the new colour to work the next stitch. Try not to pull too tightly when changing colours as this can pucker the stitches and spoil your tension (gauge). When changing colours, always feed one colour from the top and the other colour from the bottom. The yarn fed from the bottom will be more dominant in the pattern.

If you stop using one of your yarns before the end of a row, always carry it along to the end of that row. Before starting the next row, twist it in with the colour currently in use. This will ensure that your work remains the same thickness and the ends of your knitting remain neat.

Always block your Fair Isle knitting according to the yarn used, to relax the stitches and create a neat finish. For more information, refer to the section on Blocking on pages 106 and 107.

Equipment

YARN

3 balls of DK (8-ply/light worsted) yarn; 2 balls in purple (A) and 1 ball in grey (B); 50g/104m/113yd

KNITTING NEEDLES

3.25mm needles (UK 10, US 3)
4mm needles (UK 8, US 6)

TENSION (GAUGE)

Approx. 25 sts and 28 rows measure 10 x 10cm (4 x 4in) in stocking (stockinette) stitch over pattern using 4mm (UK 8, US 6) needles, unstretched

MEASUREMENTS

Mug Cosy: to fit a 10cm (4in) tall mug with a 25cm (9¾in) circumference and a gap of 1cm (½in) between the top and bottom of the mug and the handle

Tea Cosy: to fit a medium (4-cup) teapot that is approx. 16.5–17.5cm (6½–7in) high

Yarn notes

I used King Cole Merino Blend DK, a 100% superwash wool. The colours I used are Magenta (793) and Pewter (1528).

Fair Isle (stranded)

Fair Isle is a technique for working two (or more) colours of yarn in the same row while repeating a pattern. Yarn not being used is carried along the back of the work, which is called 'stranding'.

Traditional Fair Isle only uses two colours at a time. Patterns are usually repetitive, so they're easy to remember once you get going.

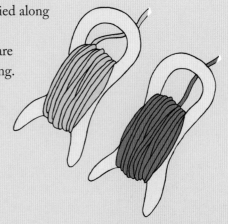

Showing Fair Isle pattern on the right side of knitting

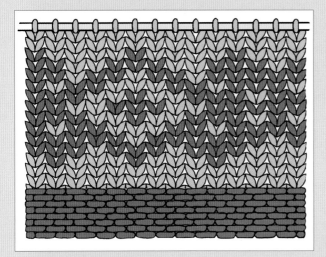

Showing Fair Isle stranding on the wrong side of knitting

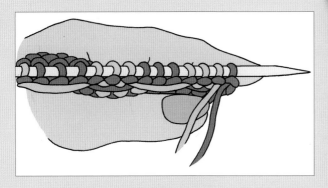

Tea Cosy pattern

Front and back (make 2)

Using 3.25mm (UK 10, US 3) needles and yarn A, cast on 57 sts.

Row 1: (K1, P1) to the last st, K1.

Row 2: (P1, K1) to the last st, P1.

Rows 3–8: rep rows 1 and 2 another three times.

Change to 4mm (UK 8, US 6) needles and join yarn B.

Row 1: work row 1 of chart (see page 74).

Row 2: work row 2 of chart, knitting the first and last sts.

Rows 3–30: work corresponding rows of chart (working in st st and knitting first and last st on purl rows).

Cut yarn B, continue in yarn A.

Rows 31–42: starting with a K row, work 12 rows in st st.

Row 43 (eyelet row): K2, Yfwd, K2tog, (K1, Yfwd, K2tog) to the last 2 sts, K2tog (56 sts).

Rows 44–48: starting with a P row, work 5 rows in st st.

Next work a picot cast-off as follows:

Knit first 2 sts, lift the second st on the right needle over the first st to cast off. *Pass the st on the right needle back to the left needle, cast on 2 sts using a 2-needle cast on method, cast off 4 sts. Rep from * to last st. Cast off. Cut yarn and pull through last st on needle.

To finish

Spray block (see Techniques, page 106), pin flat and leave to dry completely. Stitch the bottom edges of the cosy together at the ribbed edges. Stitch the top edges together down to the last Fair Isle row (Row 30). Weave all yarn ends into WS of work and trim. Make a twisted cord as follows:

Take a length of yarn 4m (4¼yd) long. Fold the yarn in half and place the folded loop around a door handle, or pin it securely to a pillow. Knot the two yarn ends together and place a pencil in this loop. Pull the yarn tight and start turning the pencil so that the yarn begins to twist. Keep going until the twists are really tight and the cord starts to kink when the pencil is relaxed. Lift the yarn off the door handle or pillow carefully, so that it doesn't unwind. Fold the cord in half, letting it twist around itself to make a thicker cord and knot the two ends together. Thread the cord through the eyelet holes and tie in a bow. If necessary, knot the ends of the cord nearer to the bow and trim ends below the knots.

Chart for tea cosy

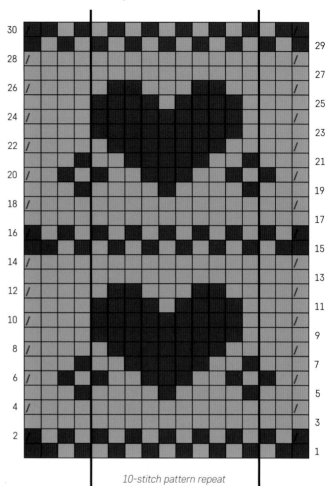

10-stitch pattern repeat

About the yarn

King Cole Merino Blend DK yarn is soft and great to knit with. The yarn is a 'superwash' wool, so you can machine wash it, which makes it perfect for projects that need regular washing, such as this tea cosy and mug cosy set. It comes in a wide range of colours, so you're sure to find your favourite. You can substitute any DK (8-ply/light worsted) weight yarn with a similar yardage.

Mug Cosy pattern

Using yarn A and 3.25mm (UK 10, US 3) needles, cast on 57 sts.

Row 1 (RS): (K1, P1) to the last st, K1.

Row 2: (P1, K1) to the last st, P1.

Change to 4mm (UK 8, US 6) needles and join yarn B.

Row 1: work row 1 of chart.

Row 2: work row 2 of chart, knitting the first and last st.

Rows 3–16: continue to work corresponding rows of chart (working in st st and knitting first and last st on purl rows).

Cut yarn B and continue in yarn A.

Row 17: K.

Change to 3.25mm (UK 10, US 3) needles to work final two rows of rib pattern.

Row 18: (P1, K1) to the last st, P1.

Row 19: (K1, P1) to the last st, K1.

Cast off following rib pattern in row 18. Fasten off and weave in ends.

To finish

Spray block, pin flat and leave to dry completely. Stitch the top and bottom edges of the cosy together at the ribbed edge for 1cm (½in). Weave all yarn ends into WS of work and trim.

Switch colours to make a second matching mug cosy, using grey as yarn A and purple as yarn B.

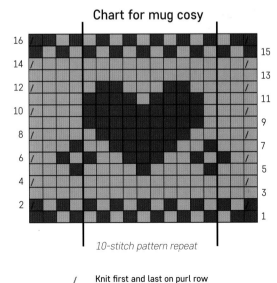

Chart for mug cosy

10-stitch pattern repeat

 /   Knit first and last on purl row

■   Yarn A

■   Yarn B

Cabled Fingerless Mittens

Learning new skills at the same time as creating stunning accessories is a win-win scenario. Your friends will love your cabled fingerless mittens, so you may find yourself knitting more. The step-by-step tutorial on how to do cable stitch (shown opposite) is quick and easy to follow, if you've never done it before.

Cable knitting notes

To make a cable, you place a specified number of stitches onto a cable needle, which is a tool that is used to hold your stitches, either at the front or the back of your work. These short needles are pointed at both ends and can be straight or hooked. The cable needle should be the same size as your knitting needles (or smaller). Do not use a larger needle as this will stretch the stitches and make them loose.

Depending on whether you hold the cable needle at the front or back of your work will determine the way that your cables will lean. Holding the cable needle at the front of your work will create a left-leaning cable, whereas holding the cable needle at the back of your work will create a right-leaning cable.

Cables are usually worked on a background of reverse stocking (stockinette) stitch, and the number of stitches used can vary. Always read your knitting abbreviations to make sure that you use the correct number of stitches as stated in your pattern.

You will see abbreviations like C4F and C4B or C6F and C6B. The C before the number tells you that these stitches are cable stitches. The number tells you how many stitches in total are involved with this particular cable movement. The F or B indicates whether you should hold the stitches to the front (F) or to the back (B) of your work.

Equipment

YARN
1 ball of DK (8-ply/light worsted) yarn in variegated; 100g/294m/322yd

KNITTING NEEDLES
4mm (UK 8, US 6)
4.5mm (UK 7, US 7)
4mm (UK 8, US 6) cable needle

OTHER ITEMS
2 stitch markers

TENSION (GAUGE)
24 sts and 32 rows to 10 x 10cm (4 x 4in) in stocking (stockinette) stitch using 4mm (UK 8, US 6) needles

22 sts and 28 rows to 10 x 10cm (4 x 4in) in stocking (stockinette) stitch using 4.5mm (UK 7, US 7) needles

MEASUREMENTS
By using different-sized needles for the main hand, these can be made to fit a small/medium hand (18–19cm (7–7½in)) or a medium/large hand (19–20cm (7½–8in))

Yarn notes

I used King Cole Riot DK, a yarn with a 70% acrylic and 30% wool mix. The colour I used is Foliage (1689).

Cable Stitch

When working cable stitches, you cross a group of stitches across each other and, depending on the way you do this, you can create a whole variety of attractive criss-cross patterns and textures that look like twisting ropes.

To make a simple cable that crosses at the front over 4 stitches (C4F):

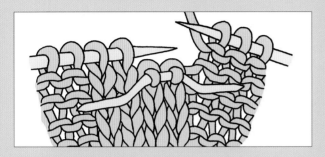

1 When you've reached the correct point along the row being worked, place the next 2 stitches onto a cable needle and leave them at the front of your knitting.

2 Knit the next 2 stitches from the left-hand needle.

3 Let go of the left-hand needle and hold the cable needle. Knit the 2 stitches from the cable needle in the same order as they came off the needle. Your cable is now complete and your stitches are crossed.

To make a simple cable that crosses at the back over 4 stitches (C4B):

To create a back cross cable over 4 stitches (C4B), simply repeat all instructions above, but at Step 1 leave the cable needle at the back of your knitting instead of at the front.

Cabled Fingerless Mittens pattern

Right mitten

Using yarn A and 4.5mm (UK 7, US 7) needles, cast on 43 sts.

Lower rib

Row 1: (P1, K2) to the last st, P1.

Row 2: (K1, P2) to the last st, K1.

Rows 3–8: rep rows 1 and 2 another three times.

Row 1: P1, K2, P1, place marker, M1, K14, place marker, work rib row 1 to end (44 sts).

Row 2: work rib row 2 to marker, slip marker, P to next marker, slip marker, K1, P2, K1.

Row 3: P1, K2, P1, slip marker, K3, (C6F) twice, slip marker, work rib row 1 to end.

Row 4: rep row 2.

Row 5: P1, K2, P1, slip marker, K to next marker, slip marker, work rib row 1 to end.

Row 6: rep row 2.

Row 7: P1, K2, P1, slip marker, (C6B) twice, K3, slip marker, work rib row 1 to end.

Row 8: rep row 2.

Row 9: P1, K2, P1, slip marker, K to next marker, slip marker, work rib row 1 to end.

Rows 10–16: rep rows 2–8.

Change to 4mm (UK 8, US 6) needles for small/medium size or continue with 4.5mm (UK 7, US 7) needles for medium/large size.

Rep rows 9–16 twice more, or for a shorter mitten, continue with thumb shaping.

Thumb shaping

Keeping rib pattern correct (P the purl stitches and K the knit stitches):

Row 1: rib to marker, slip marker, K to next marker, slip marker, rib to end.

Row 2: rib to marker, slip marker, P to next marker, slip marker, rib to end.

Row 3: rib to marker, slip marker, K3, (C6F) twice, slip marker, P1, K2, P1, M1, K to end (45 sts).

Row 4: P to 4 sts before marker, K1, P2, K1, slip marker, P to next marker, slip marker, rib to end.

Row 5: rib to marker, slip marker, K to next marker, slip marker, P1, K2, P1, K to end.

Row 6: rep row 4.

Row 7: rib to marker, slip marker, (C6B) twice, K3, slip marker, P1, K2, P1, M1, K1, M1, K to end (47 sts).

Rows 8–10: rep rows 4–6.

Row 11: rib to marker, slip marker, K3, (C6F) twice, slip marker, P1, K2, P1, M1, K3, M1, K to end (49 sts).

Rows 12–14: rep rows 4–6.

Row 15: rib to marker, slip marker, (C6B) twice, K3, slip marker, P1, K2, P1, M1, K5, M1, K to end (51 sts).

Rows 16–18: rep rows 4–6.

Row 19: rib to marker, slip marker, K3, (C6F) twice, slip marker, P1, K2, P1, M1, K7, M1, K to end (53 sts).

Rows 20–22: rep rows 4–6.

Row 23: rib to marker, slip marker, (C6B) twice, K3, slip marker, P1, K2, P1, M1, K9, M1, K to end (55 sts).

Rows 24–26: rep rows 4–6.

Row 27: rib to marker, slip marker, K3, (C6F) twice, slip marker, P1, K2, P1, M1, K11, M1, K to end (57 sts).

Row 28: rep row 4.

Thumb

Row 1: rib to marker, slip marker, k to next marker, P1, K2, P1, K13, turn. **Slip remaining sts from left needle sts onto a stitch holder (the remaining stitches and stitch marker on the right needle can remain on the right needle while knitting the thumb).

Row 2: cast on 2 sts, P15, turn.

Row 3: cast on 2 sts, K17, turn.

Rows 4–6: starting with a P row, work 3 rows in stocking (stockinette) stitch.

Row 7: (K1, P1) to the last st, K1.

Row 8: (P1, K1) to the last st, P1.

Cast off in K1, P1 rib pattern. Sew thumb seam.

Slide the sts from the stitch holder back to the empty needle**.

Pick up and knit 5 sts across the bottom of the thumb, K to end (49 sts).

Next Row: P to 6 sts before marker, P2tog, K1, P2, K1, slip marker, P to next marker, slip marker, rib to end (48 sts).

Hand

Row 1: rib to marker, slip marker, (C6B) twice, K3, slip marker, (P1, K2) twice, K2tog, K to end (47 sts).

Row 2: P to 4 sts before marker, K1, P2, K1, slip marker, p to next marker, slip marker, rib to end.

Row 3: rib to marker, slip marker, K to next marker, slip marker, P1, K2, P1, K to end.

Row 4: rep row 2.

Row 5: rib to marker, slip marker, K3, (C6F) twice, slip marker, P1, K2, P1, K to end.

Rows 6–8: rep rows 2–4.

Row 9: rib to marker, slip marker, (C6B) twice, K3, slip marker, P1, K2, P1, K to end.

Row 10: rep row 2.

Upper rib

Row 1: P1, K2, P1, K2tog, K1, P1, (K2, P1) to the end (46 sts).

Row 2: (K1, P2) to the last st, K1.

Row 3: (P1, K2) to the last st, P1.

Row 4: (K1, P2) to the last st, K1.

Rep rows 3 and 4 twice more.

Cast off in rib. Cut yarn leaving a 30cm (12in) tail end and pull through last st on needle.

To finish

Use yarn ends to stitch the side seam using mattress stitch for an invisible finish.

Left mitten

Using yarn A and 4.5mm (UK 7, US 7) needles, cast on 43 sts.

Lower rib

Row 1: (P1, K2) to the last st, P1.

Row 2: (K1, P2) to the last st, K1.

Rows 3–8: rep rows 1 and 2 another three times.

Row 1: (P1, K2) 8 times, P1, place marker, K14, M1, place marker, work Rib Row 1 to end (44 sts).

Row 2: work rib row 2 to marker, slip marker, P to next marker, slip marker, work rib row 2 to end.

Row 3: work rib row 1 to marker, slip marker, (C6B) twice, K3, slip marker, work rib row 1 to end.

Row 4: rep row 2.

Row 5: work rib row 1 to marker, slip marker, K to next marker, slip marker, work rib row 1 to end.

Row 6: rep row 2.

Row 7: work rib row 1 to marker, slip marker, K3, (C6F) twice, slip marker, work rib row 1 to end.

Row 8: rep row 2.

Row 9: work rib row 1 to marker, slip marker, K to next marker, slip marker, work rib row 1 to end.

Rows 10–16: rep rows 2–8.

Change to 4mm (UK 8, US 6) needles for small/medium size or continue with 4.5mm (UK 7, US 7) needles for medium/ large size.

Rep rows 9–16 twice more, or for a shorter mitten, continue with thumb shaping.

Thumb shaping

Keeping rib pattern correct (P the purl stitches and K the knit stitches):

Row 1: rib to marker, slip marker, K to next marker, slip marker, rib to end.

Row 2: rib to marker, slip marker, P to next marker, slip marker, rib to end.

Row 3: K to 4 sts before marker, M1, P1, K2, P1, slip marker, (C6B) twice, K3, slip marker, rib to end (45 sts).

Row 4: rib to marker, slip marker, p to next marker, slip marker, K1, P2, K1, P to end.

Row 5: K to 4 sts before marker, P1, K2, P1, slip marker, K to next marker, slip marker, rib to end.

Row 6: rep row 4.

Row 7: K to 5 sts before marker, M1, K1, M1, P1, K2, P1, slip marker, K3, (C6F) twice, slip marker, rib to end (47 sts).

Rows 8–10: rep rows 4–6.

Row 11: K to 7 sts before marker, M1, K3, M1, P1, K2, P1, slip marker, (C6B) twice, K3, slip marker, rib to end (49 sts).

Rows 12–14: rep rows 4–6.

Row 15: K to 9 sts before marker, M1, K5, M1, P1, K2, P1, slip marker, K3, (C6F) twice, slip marker, rib to end (51 sts).

Rows 16–18: rep rows 4–6.

Row 19: K to 11 sts before marker, M1, K7, M1, P1, K2, P1, slip marker, (C6B) twice, K3, slip marker, rib to end (53 sts).

Rows 20–22: rep rows 4–6.

Row 23: K to 13 sts before marker, M1, K9, M1, P1, K2, P1, slip marker, K3, (C6F) twice, slip marker, rib to end (55 sts).

Rows 24–26: rep rows 4–6.

Row 27: K to 15 sts before marker, M1, K11, M1, P1, K2, P1, slip marker, (C6B) twice, K3, slip marker, rib to end (57 sts).

Row 28: rep row 4.

Thumb

Row 1: K to 4 sts before marker, turn.

Work from ** to ** as given for Right Hand thumb.

Pick up and knit 5 sts from thumb seam, P1, K2, P1, slip marker, K to next marker, slip marker, rib to end (49 sts).

Next row: rib to marker, slip marker, P to next marker, slip marker, K1, P2, K1, P2tog, P to end (48 sts).

Hand

Row 1: K to 8 sts before marker, K2tog, (K2, P1) twice, slip marker, K3, (C6F) twice, slip marker, rib to end (47 sts).

Row 2: rib to marker, slip marker, P to next marker, slip marker, K1, P2, K1, P to end.

Row 3: K to 4 sts before marker, P1, K2, P1, slip marker, K to next marker, slip marker, rib to end.

Row 4: rep row 2.

Row 5: K to 4 sts before marker, P1, K2, P1, slip marker, (C6B) twice, K3, slip marker, rib to end.

Rows 6–8: rep rows 2–4.

Row 9: K to 4 sts before marker, P1, K2, P1, slip marker, K3, (C6F) twice, slip marker, rib to end.

Row 10: rep row 2.

Upper rib

Row 1: (P1, K2) 13 times, P1, K2tog, K1, P1, K2, P1 (46 sts).

Row 2: (K1, P2) to the last st, K1.

Row 3: (P1, K2) to the last st, P1.

Row 4: (K1, P2) to the last st, K1.

Rep rows 3 and 4 twice more.

Cast off in rib. Cut yarn leaving a 30cm (12in) tail end and pull through last stitch on needle.

To finish

Use yarn ends to stitch the side seam using mattress stitch for an invisible finish.

Evening Purse

Combining knit and purl stitches with slipped stitches can create more complicated patterns to great effect. By using extra special luxury yarn, this purse is definitely good enough for a glamorous night out.

Evening Purse pattern

Front and back (make 2)

Cast on 65 sts.

Row 1 (RS): K4, (yf, sl3 wyf, yb, K3) to last st, K1.

Row 2: K1, sl1 wyb, yf, (P3, yb, sl3 wyb, yf) to last 3 sts, P2, K1.

Row 3: K2, (yf, sl3 wyf, yb, K3) to last 3 sts, yf, sl2 wyf, yb, K1.

Row 4: K1, (sl3 wyb, yf, P3, yb) to last 4 sts, sl3 wyb, K1.

Row 5: K1, yf, sl2 wyf, yb, (K3, yf, sl3 wyf, yb) to last 2 sts, K2.

Row 6: K1, yf, P2, (yb, sl3 wyb, yf, P3) to last 2 sts, yb, sl1 wyb, K1.

Row 7: rep row 1.

Row 8: rep row 2.

Row 9: rep row 3.

Row 10: rep row 4.

Row 11: rep row 3.

Row 12: rep row 2.

Row 13: rep row 1.

Row 14: rep row 6.

Row 15: rep row 5.

Row 16: rep row 4.

Row 17: rep row 3.

Row 18: rep row 2.

Row 19: rep row 1.

Row 20: rep row 6.

Rows 21–136: work rows 1–20 of pattern 5 times more then rep Rows 1–16 of pattern.

Row 137: K2tog, (yf, sl3 wyf, yb, K3) to last 3 sts, yf, sl1 wyf, yb, K2tog (63 sts).

Row 138: P2tog, P2, (yb, sl3 wyb, yf, p3) to last 5 sts, yb, sl3 wyb, yf, P2tog (61 sts).

Row 139: K2tog, (yf, sl3 wyf, yb, K3) to last 5 sts, yf, sl3 wyf, yb, K2tog (59 sts).

Row 140: P2tog, yb, sl1 wyb, yf, (P3, yb, sl3 wyb, yf) to last 2 sts, P2tog (57 sts).

Cast off.

Equipment

YARN
2 balls of DK (8-ply/light worsted) yarn in blue; 50g/120m/131yd

KNITTING NEEDLES
4mm (UK 8, US 6)

OTHER ITEMS
0.5m (½yd) lining fabric, sewing needle and thread

1 x 20cm (8in) purse frame with loops, either sew-in or glue-in

Glue gun (if needed for frame)

Purse chain approx. 1m (39½in) long

TENSION (GAUGE)
Approx. 32.5 sts and 66 rows measure 10 x 10 cm (4 x 4 in) in slip stitch herringbone pattern using 4mm (UK 8, US 6) needles

MEASUREMENTS
Approx. 20cm wide x 22cm long (8 x 8½in)

Yarn notes

I used Erika Knight Studio Linen, a mix of 85% recycled rayon linen and 15% premium linen. The colour I used is Neo (8).

To finish

Spray block the front and back pieces (see Techniques, page 106), pin pieces out to 21 x 22cm (8¼ x 8½in) and leave to dry completely.

Using each knitted piece as a template, cut out 2 pieces of contrast fabric with a 1cm (½in) seam allowance all around. Fold 1cm (½in) hem of fabric to WS and iron. Whip stitch lining to WS of each knitted piece.

Carefully glue or sew the top of each piece to the purse frame (the shaped edge/cast-off edge).

When attaching the frame, use small dabs of glue at a time because the glue will dry very quickly. Starting from the centre of the frame squeeze a small dab of glue into the purse frame channel, push the fabric into the channel and leave to dry. Repeat this process along the frame, working small areas at a time, then repeat for the opposite side of the frame. If you use a sew-in frame, use matching sewing thread, doubled for strength, and start from the centre, working outwards.

Sew around the side and bottom seams using mattress stitch and matching yarn (working from the RS). Weave all ends into WS and trim. Attach the chain to the loops on the purse frame.

About the yarn

This evening purse is knitted in Erika Knight Studio Linen, a soft and durable yarn. It gives a clear stitch definition so it really complements the slip stitch pattern. There are eight beautiful colours to choose from. You can substitute any DK (8-ply/light worsted) yarn that is linen, bamboo, cotton or silk.

Hot Water Bottle

Curl up with a hot water bottle on a cold winter's night and you'll be warm and cosy in no time. Personalise your cover with duplicate stitch to create a slightly textured and bold effect. Use it to stand out from the crowd!

Hot Water Bottle pattern

Front

Lower rib

Using yarn A and 3.5mm (no UK equivalent, US 4) needles, cast on 53 sts.

Row 1: (K1, P1) to the last st, K1.

Row 2: (P1, K1) to the last st, P1.

Rows 3–20: rep rows 1 and 2 nine times more, increasing 1 st at the end of the last row (do this by Pfb in the last st) (54 sts). Continue with Main body.

Main body

Change to 3.25mm (UK 10, US 3) needles. Work 74 rows in st st, placing a stitch marker on the 16th st of row 27.

Neck shaping

Row 75: K1, skpo, K to last 3 sts, K2tog, K1 (52 sts).

Row 76: P.

Rows 77–78: rep rows 75 and 76 once more (50 sts).

Equipment

YARN

3 balls of DK (8-ply/light worsted) yarn; 2 balls in cream (A), 1 ball in grey (B) and oddments of red (C); 50g/120m/131yd

KNITTING NEEDLES

3.5mm (no UK equivalent, US 4) 3.25mm (UK 10, US 3)

OTHER ITEMS

A standard 2L hot water bottle that is 18.5cm wide and 28cm from base to start of neck (7¼ x 11in)

TENSION (GAUGE)

27 sts and 37 rows measure 10 x 10cm (4 x 4in) in st st using 3.25mm (UK 10, US 3) needles

MEASUREMENTS

19.5cm (8in) wide and 28cm (11in) from base to start of neck ribbing when stretched over the bottle; to fit standard 2L hot water bottle

Yarn notes

I used Sublime Superfine Alpaca, a 100% alpaca yarn. The colours I used are Tusk (430), Flannel (434) (oddments only) and a 2m (2yd) length of Taylor (460).

Duplicate Stitch

Duplicate stitch (also known as Swiss darning) allows you to add small areas of colour to your knitting, duplicating the original stitches. It creates a slightly raised effect.

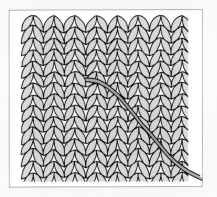

1 Thread your needle with a long piece of the contrast yarn and bring it up through the point of the 'V' of the first stitch being duplicated.

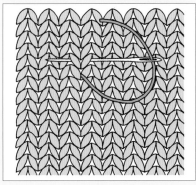

2 Take the needle under the 'V' of the stitch above it.

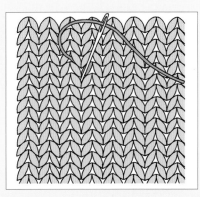

3 Take the needle back through the point of the 'V' being worked. One stitch has been duplicated.

4 Repeat across the row for each area of colour, following any charts provided.

Row 79: K1, skpo, (2 sts on right-hand needle) lift the second stitch on the right needle over the first stitch to cast off 1 stitch then cast off 4 more sts, K to last 3 sts, K2tog, K1 (43 sts).

Row 80: cast off 5 sts, P to the end (38 sts).

Row 81: cast off 3 sts, K to the end (35 sts).

Row 82: cast off 3 sts, P to the end (32 sts).

Rows 83–84: rep rows 81 and 82 once more, decreasing 1 st at the end of row 84 (do this by P2tog over the last 2 sts) (25 sts).

Change to 3.5mm (no UK equivalent, US 4) needles and continue with Neck rib.

Neck rib

Row 1: (K1, P1) to the last st, K1.

Row 2: (P1, K1) to the last st, P1.

Rows 3–24: rep rows 1 and 2 eleven times more (or until long enough to cover neck of hot water bottle). Cast off in rib, leaving a long tail of yarn.

Back

Follow all instructions as given for Front, omitting the stitch marker.

Duplicate stitch

Using the chart below, use duplicate stitch (or Swiss darning) to stitch the motif onto the stocking (stockinette) stitch base, using yarn B and yarn C. Start at the marked stitch (on row 27).

Begin at the bottom right corner of the chart and work in rows.

To finish

Spray block pieces (see Techniques, page 106) and leave to dry completely. Sew the side seams using mattress stitch and place on hot water bottle.

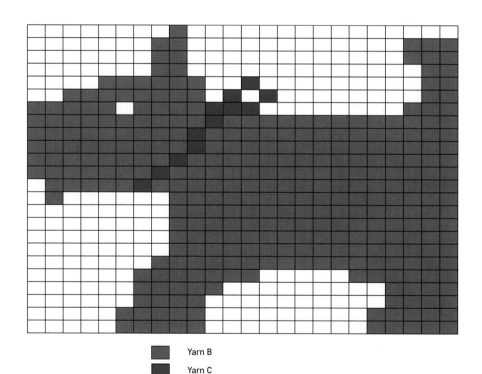

■ Yarn B
■ Yarn C

About the yarn

Sublime Superfine Alpaca DK is beautifully soft and luxurious. The yarn is cool in summer and snuggly in winter and the colour palette is warm and cosy too. Sublime Superfine Alpaca DK has a standard DK (8-ply/light worsted) tension (gauge) so you can substitute any similar yarn of your choice.

Essential Techniques

Tension (gauge)

Tension (gauge) is critical in knitting when you need to achieve a desired size, such as when knitting a garment, hat or socks. Tension (gauge) refers to the size of your stitches, which in turn affects the size of your finished project.

Every knitting pattern should state the tension (gauge) that you need to achieve in order to make your project to the correct size, using a given size of needles and yarn type or weight. If you don't knit to the tension (gauge) stated, your finished project won't match the dimensions in the pattern.

If you knit a looser stitch or tension (gauge), your finished project will turn out larger than the pattern dimensions. On the other hand, if you knit a tighter stitch or tension (gauge), your finished product will turn out smaller than the pattern dimensions. This can be devastating, especially if you've spent months knitting a jumper, only to find that it's far too big or small. So it's important to check that you knit to the same tension (gauge) as given in the pattern, before you start knitting your project.

1 Cast on at least 10 more stitches than specified on the ball band tension (gauge) for a 10 x 10cm (4 x 4in) square, and knit at least 10 more rows than instructed. Knit in stocking (stockinette) stitch, or in the pattern stated within the instructions. Cast off loosely so that the top few rows of knitting are not distorted.

2 Lay the square on a flat surface. Place a see-through ruler vertically across the square and measure 10cm (4in) across the centre of the square. Mark the beginning and end of the 10cm (4in) length with pins (see top right).

3 Do the same vertically and place pins as markers (see bottom right).

4 Count how many stitches and how many rows there are between the pins. This is your tension (gauge) for the yarn and needles used.

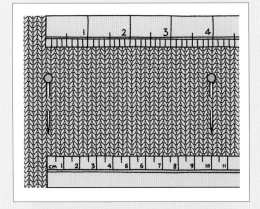

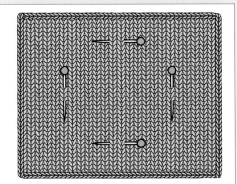

If your stitch and row counts are the same as specified by the pattern, you can go ahead and start knitting. If you have more stitches and rows, you are knitting too tightly and your project will end up too small. You'll need to make another swatch with slightly larger needles and measure again.

If you have fewer stitches than specified, you are knitting too loosely and your project will be too big. You'll need to make another swatch with slightly smaller needles and measure again.

Continue to swatch with different-sized needles until you achieve the correct tension (gauge) stated in the pattern.

Casting on

Cable cast on

This method uses two needles and is very similar to the knit stitch and is sometimes called 'knitting on'.

1 Make a slip knot onto one needle, leaving a short tail of yarn (long enough to weave into your work when finished). Hold in your left hand.

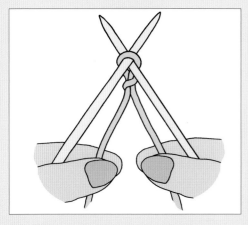

2 Insert the other needle into the stitch, from the front, as if to knit and form an 'x' with the needles.

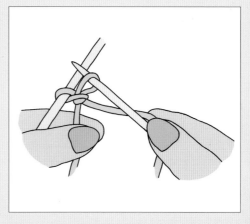

3 Wrap the yarn from the yarn ball around the back needle and pull the new loop back through, just as if you were making a knit stitch.

4 Move the loop that has just been made to the left-hand needle by slipping the left-hand needle into the loop from the front. Then slide the right-hand needle out of the stitch. You now have two stitches on the left-hand needle.

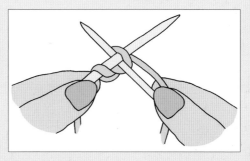

5 To create the rest of the stitches, insert the needle in between the last stitch made and the one before it (not into the loop) and repeat steps 3 and 4 until you have the required number of stitches.

Casting on (continued)

Long tail cast on

This method uses a long yarn tail and one needle. It creates an edge that has great elasticity and is perfect for edges that need to be very stretchy.

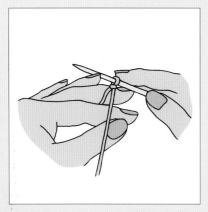

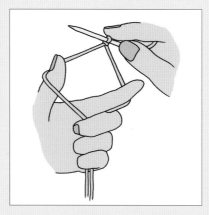

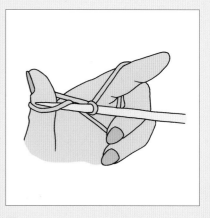

1 Make a slip knot onto one needle, leaving a tail of yarn that is approximately 3–5 times longer than the desired cast-on edge. Hold the needle in your right hand. Place your thumb and index finger between the 2 strands of yarn with the working yarn falling behind the index finger and the tail end in front of the thumb.

2 Grasp the loose ends of yarn with your other fingers and hold in palm. Spread your thumb and forefinger apart to make a diamond shape with the yarn and keeping yarn taut. Move your thumb up towards the tip of the needle, keeping your palm facing forwards.

3 Bring the needle downwards then up through the loop on the thumb, from the bottom.

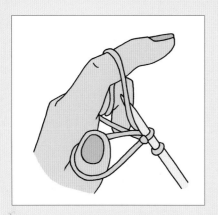

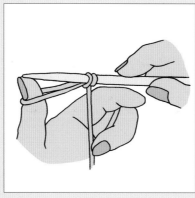

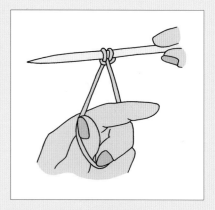

4 Take needle under the yarn from the index finger.

5 Take the needle back through the thumb loop (insert from the top).

6 Carefully remove thumb from loop and pull gently on yarn ends to tighten the stitch. Repeat until you have cast on the number of stitches indicated in the pattern.

Casting off

Once your knitting is finished you will need to cast your stitches off the needle. To prevent your cast-off edge becoming too tight, you can use a knitting needle that is one or two sizes bigger than the ones used for the body of your knitting.

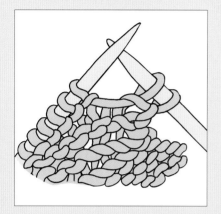

1 Knit the next 2 stitches (2 stitches now on right-hand needle).

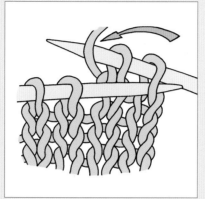

2 Insert the tip of the left-hand needle into the first stitch on the right needle (the stitch at the bottom). Lift the bottom stitch over the top stitch, then over the tip of the right-hand needle and drop it off the needle.

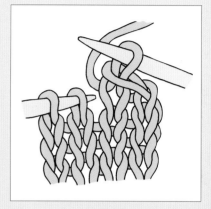

3 The stitch now remains on the right-hand needle.

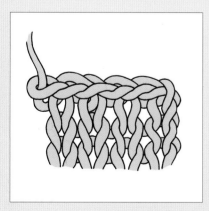

4 Knit the next stitch, then repeat steps 2 and 3 until all stitches are cast off. Cut yarn and pull it through the last stitch, leaving a long enough tail to weave in later.

NOTE
To cast off purlwise (as if to purl) follow all steps above, but purl all stitches instead of knitting them.

Basic Stitches

Knit

Knit and Purl are the two stitches that form the basis of all stitch patterns. The standard abbreviation for Knit in a pattern is K.

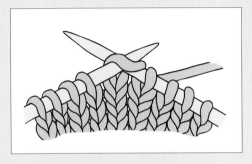

1 With the yarn at back of your work, insert the right-hand needle through the first stitch on the left-hand needle from the front to the back, forming an 'x' with the needles.

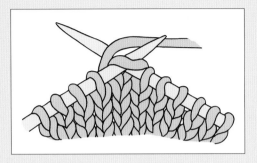

2 Wrap the yarn around the right-hand needle.

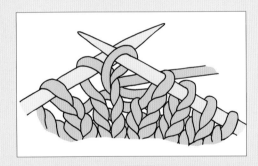

3 Pull a loop through to the front of your work.

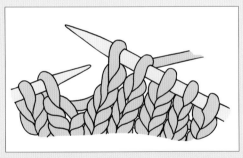

4 Slip the original stitch off the left-hand needle, leaving the newly formed stitch on the right-hand needle. The yarn is still at the back of the work. Repeat steps 1–4 until all stitches on the left-hand needle have been transferred to the right-hand needle.

Purl

The standard abbreviation for Purl in a pattern is P.

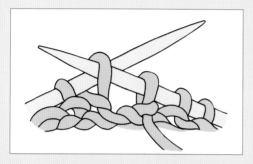

1 With yarn at front of work, insert the right-hand needle through the first stitch on the left-hand needle from the back to the front, forming an 'x', with the right-hand needle at the front.

2 Wrap the yarn around the right-hand needle.

3 Draw a loop through to the back of work.

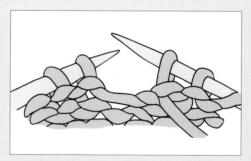

4 Slip the original stitch off the left-hand needle, leaving the newly formed stitch on the right-hand needle. Yarn is still at front of work. Repeat steps 1–4 until all stitches on the left-hand needle have been transferred to the right-hand needle.

Increasing

Increasing allows you to shape your knitting and there are two main increasing methods used in knitting: M1 (make 1 stitch) and Kfb (knit front and back).

Make 1 stitch (M1)

This stitch can slant to the left or the right. This increase method is the least visible. Increases are made by knitting into the horizontal bar lying between the two needles. One method creates an increase leaning slightly to the left (M1L) and the other creates an increase leaning slightly to the right (M1R).

Method 1 (M1L)

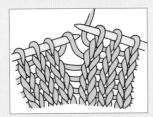 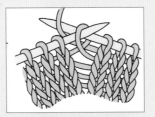

1 Insert the tip of the left-hand needle from front to back into the horizontal bar lying between the two needles.

2 Insert the right-hand needle into the back of the loop and knit the stitch. Knitting into the back of the loop twists the stitch and avoids making a hole. Slip the strand off the left-hand needle to leave a new stitch (an increase) on the right-hand needle. The new stitch slants slightly to the left.

Method 2 (M1R)

1 To make an increase that slants slightly to the right, insert the tip of the left-hand needle from back to front into the horizontal bar lying between the two needles.

2 Insert the right-hand needle into the front of the loop and knit the stitch. Knitting into the front of the loop twists the stitch and avoids making a hole. Slip the strand off the left-hand needle to leave a new stitch (an increase) on the right-hand needle. The new stitch slants slightly to the right.

Knit front and back (Kfb)

This method is the most visible of all increases as it leaves a small bump that looks like a purl stitch. The standard abbreviation is Kfb.

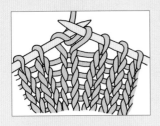

1 Knit into the next stitch as normal but do not slip the stitch off the left-hand needle.

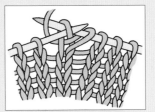

2 Take the right-hand needle to the back of work and knit into the back loop of the same stitch. Slip the stitch off the left-hand needle to leave 2 new stitches on the right-hand needle.

Decreasing

There are three main methods of decreasing one stitch. These are visible and can lean to the left or to the right. When decreases are worked at opposite ends of a row this is called 'raglan shaping' or 'fully fashioning'.

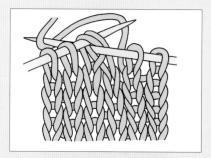

K2tog – knit 2 stitches together (leans to the right)
Insert the right-hand needle as if to knit, into the next 2 stitches on the left-hand needle (instead of 1 stitch) and then knit them together as if they were one stitch.

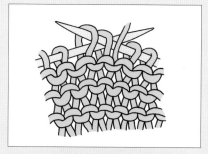

P2tog – purl 2 stitches together (leans to the right)
Insert the right-hand needle as if to purl, into the front of next 2 stitches on the left-hand needle (instead of 1 stitch) and then purl them together as if they were one stitch.

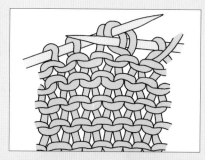

P2togtbl – purl 2 stitches together through the back loops (leans to the left)
Insert the right-hand needle purlwise (from back to front) through the back of the loops and purl them as if they were one stitch.

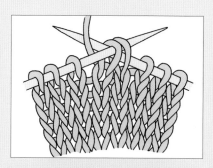

K2togtbl – knit 2 stitches together through the back loops (leans to the left)
Insert the right-hand needle knitwise (from front to back) through the back of the loops of the next two stitches on the left-hand needle and knit them as if they were one stitch.

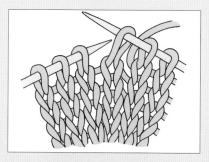

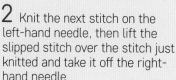

SKPO – slip one stitch, knit one stitch, pass slipped stitch over the knitted stitch (leans to the left). This is an alternative to K2togtbl.

1 Insert the right-hand needle into the next stitch on the left-hand needle (as if to knit). Slip the stitch to the right-hand needle without knitting it.

2 Knit the next stitch on the left-hand needle, then lift the slipped stitch over the stitch just knitted and take it off the right-hand needle.

Basic Stitch Patterns

Garter stitch and Stocking (stockinette) stitch are the two main stitch patterns that most people learn first when they start learning to knit.

Garter stitch

Garter stitch is the simplest of all knitting stitches. It creates a textured fabric and is very stretchy. It is formed by working every row as a knit row (follow steps 1–4 of knit stitch on page 100 for every row). The first knitted row is usually the right side (unless the pattern says otherwise). It may help to mark the right side of work with a safety pin or a small length of yarn.

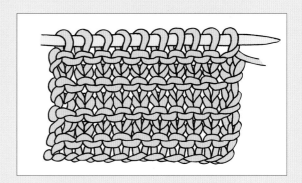

Garter stitch produces a sturdy fabric and creates a flat piece of knitting. The standard abbreviation for this stitch is g st.

Stocking (stockinette) stitch

Stocking (stockinette) stitch is created by knitting one row, then purling one row, repeated. This creates a smooth side and a bumpy side. The smooth side looks like columns of 'Vs' and is the right side. The wrong side is the textured side, which looks like bumpy ridges.

Stocking (stockinette) stitch creates a soft fabric that drapes well, and the edges will curl. This can be remedied by adding a garter stitch border. The standard abbreviation for this stitch is st st.

Right side of stocking (stockinette) stitch

Wrong side of stocking (stockinette) stitch

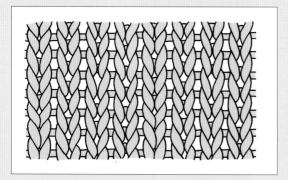

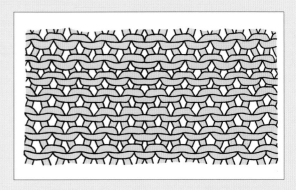

Making a Pompom

Pompoms can be made using the traditional cardboard technique, using a plastic pompom maker, or using the method below, all of which work equally well.

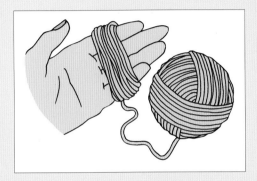

1 Wrap the yarn around your fingers (four fingers make a large pompom, three fingers make a medium pompom and two fingers make a small pompom). The more you wrap, the fuller the pompom will be.

2 Carefully slide the yarn off your fingers. Take a long piece of matching yarn and wrap it around the centre. Tie a knot in the yarn tightly, taking care not to snap the yarn. If the yarn isn't strong enough, or is too thick, use strong yarn of a similar shade. Leave the ends of the knot long and use this to attach the pompom to your project later.

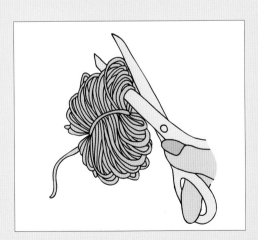

3 Use a pair of sharp scissors to cut through the folded loops on each side of the pompom.

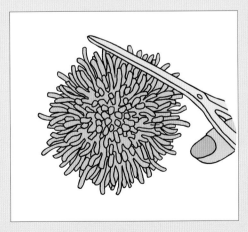

4 Give your pompom a good shake to fluff it up, then trim the ends to make a neat, rounded shape.

Blocking

Blocking describes the method of stretching, shaping and moulding a finished piece of knitting or crochet work using some form of water. It gives your work a much neater and more professional finish as it relaxes the fibres and evens out your stitches.

Blocking can also increase the size of your work to the correct size (but it cannot make your work smaller); mould your designs to a specific shape; 'open up' the designs in lacy crochet work to emphasise the stitches and patterns; help curled edges lie flat and improve the overall drape of your fabric.

There are three main methods of blocking: spray blocking, steam blocking and wet blocking, each of which is described below.

What tools and equipment do I need?

- **rust-proof pins with glass heads** (plastic heads can melt if using the steam method of blocking), or blocking pins

- **blocking wires** (optional). These can be inserted along the edges of your work to keep them straight and are often used when blocking shawls

- a **tape measure**

- a **spray bottle** filled with cold water, or a **steam iron** (or handheld steamer), or a **basin** filled with cold water

- a **towel**

- a **flat, padded surface** that is large enough to hold a piece of knitting. This could be a purpose-made folding blocking board, interlocking foam pieces, an ironing board or even a carpet covered with plastic and a towel.

Spray blocking

1 Spray your work with cold water until it is damp but not completely saturated.

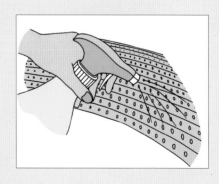

2 Using rust-proof glass-headed pins or blocking pins, pin out your knitted pieces onto a blocking board to the dimensions specified in your pattern. Gently ease the fabric into place, making sure that you do not distort the stitches. Make sure edges are straight or curved, as required.

3 Once your work is completely dry, remove the pins.

4 If the desired result is not achieved, repeat steps 1–3 again.

Steam blocking

This method is suitable for some wool fibres and cottons.

1 Follow step 1 for Spray Blocking opposite, pinning out your pieces with the wrong side up and place a clean colourfast cloth or towel over the fabric.

2 Switch on your iron or steamer and when it is hot, hold the iron close to the covered fabric and steam until it is damp. DO NOT place the iron directly onto the fabric because you will scorch the fibres and ruin your work.

3 Once your work is completely dry, remove the pins.

Wet blocking

This method is suitable for most wools, silk and other natural fibres.

1 Fill a basin or bowl with cold or lukewarm water (check the ball band for temperature instructions). If desired add a small amount of detergent (such as a wool wash or a mild shampoo). Immerse your fabric in the water to wet it.

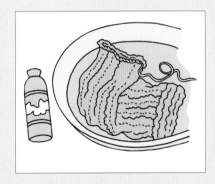

2 Lift the fabric out of the water and at the same time very carefully squeeze out the excess water. DO NOT lift the whole piece out of the water when soaking wet as your work will stretch. DO NOT wring or you will damage the fabric.

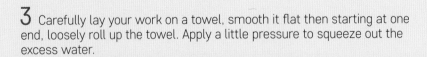

3 Carefully lay your work on a towel, smooth it flat then starting at one end, loosely roll up the towel. Apply a little pressure to squeeze out the excess water.

4 Unroll the towel then place your work onto a blocking board and pin into shape according to your pattern instructions, using rust-proof pins or blocking pins.

5 Leave to dry completely before removing the pins.

Mattress Stitch

Mattress stitch is a great technique for joining seams in knitting and creates a seam that is virtually invisible. Start with the right sides of your knitting facing up, with edges side by side.

Vertical mattress stitch

This is used for sewing row ends together.

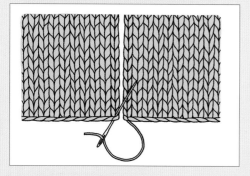

1 Thread the tail end of yarn from one piece onto a wool needle. Insert the needle up through the first cast-on or cast-off stitch on the opposite piece, from back to front.

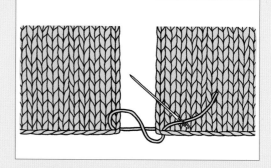

2 Insert the needle up through the corner stitch on the first piece from back to front. Pull yarn through and pull tight to bring the edges together.

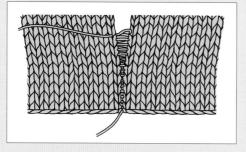

3 Take the needle across to the opposite edge again and insert it, from the front, under the horizontal bar in the middle of the outer row of stitches. Repeat step 2, working back and forth across each side, gently pulling the yarn through to close the seam. Make sure you always work along a straight line of stitches for a perfect finish.

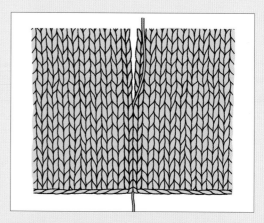

4 As you pull the yarn through, the seam closes up so that you cannot see the stitches you have just made.

Horizontal mattress stitch

This is used for seaming the cast-on or cast-off edges together.

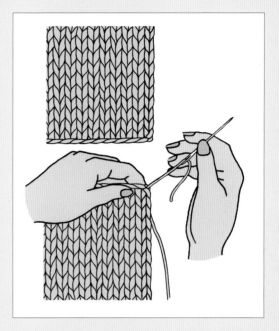

1 Place pieces with right sides up and with the cast-on and cast-off edges opposite each other.

2 Bring a threaded wool needle up through the first stitch on the bottom piece.

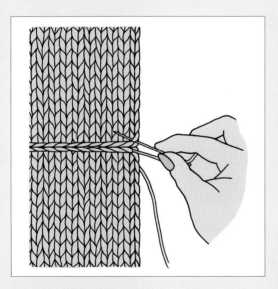

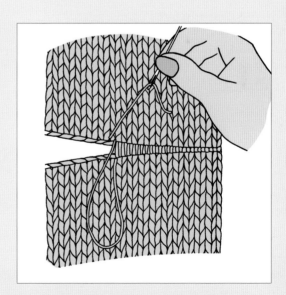

3 Take the needle across to the opposite edge and under the 'V' of the first stitch and pull the yarn through.

4 Repeat step 3, working back and forth across each side, gently pulling the yarn through to close the seam. Make sure you always work along a straight line of stitches for a perfect finish.

Abbreviations

Below is a list of the abbreviations used in the book.

cm = centimetres

C6F = slip next 3 sts onto a cable needle, hold at front of work, knit next 3 sts from left needle then knit 3 sts from cable needle

C6B = slip next 3 sts onto a cable needle, hold at back of work, knit next 3 sts from left needle then knit 3 sts from cable needle

DPN = double-pointed needle/s

g = grams

in = inch(es)

K = knit

Kfb = knit into the front then knit into the back of next stitch (to increase 1 stitch)

K2tog = knit next 2 sts together as 1 stitch (to decrease 1 stitch that slants to the right)

m = metre(s)

mm = millimetres

M1 = make 1 st (with left-hand needle pick up horizontal bar between last st and next and knit through the back of it to increase 1 stitch)

P = purl

Pfb = purl into the front then purl into the back of the next stitch (to increase 1 stitch)

rep = repeat

RS = right side

skpo = slip next st, knit next st, pass the slipped stitch over the knitted stitch (to decrease 1 stitch that slants to the left)

sl = slip next stitch (do this by inserting the right needle purlwise into the next stitch on left-hand needle. Do not knit the stitch, instead, slide it from the left to the right-hand needle)

st(s) = stitch(es)

WS = wrong side

wyb = with yarn at back

wyf = with yarn at front

yb = yarn back (take yarn to back between the 2 needles and not around the needle)

yd = yard(s)

yf = yarn forward (bring yarn to front between the 2 needles and not around the needle)

yfwd = bring yarn between needles to the front of work and round the right-hand needle to the back of work (to increase 1 stitch)

yrn = wrap yarn around needle (to increase 1 stitch)

( ) = repeat all instructions within round brackets as many times as stated

[ ] = larger sizes in square brackets

* = indicates the start of a repeat sequence, to be repeated as many times as stated

Yarn conversions

UK	US	Australia
4-ply	fingering	4-ply
DK or 8-ply	DK or light worsted	8-ply
aran	worsted	10-ply

Index

B
bag handles 17
ball-winder 17
basic stitches
  knit 100
  purl 101
basic stitch patterns
  garter stitch 104
  stocking (stockinette) stitch 104
basketweave 47
bunting 48

C
cabled fingerless mittens 17, 78
casting on
  cable cast on 97
  long tail cast on 98
chunky pillows 26
colour block cowl 34

D
dot stitch 47

E
evening purse 86

F
fabric pieces 17
family hats 30

G
gauge (see tension)

H
hot water bottle 90

I
insomnia 28

J
Jon Kabat-Zinn 8

K
knitting needles 14–15
  circular 15

  conversion chart 15
  double-pointed 15
  size gauge 17
  straight 15
knitting, therapeutic 8, 12

L
love hearts tea cosy set 72

M
mindfulness 8
mug cosies 77

N
notebook 17
nursery blanket 58

P
parachute, weaving your 8
patchwork blanket 44
pen 17
pins, rust-proof 17, 106
pompom makers 17, 105
project bag 17
purse frames 17, 86

R
ribbon 17
row counter 17
ruler 15

S
scissors 15
sewing needle 17
sewing thread 17
shawl 62
sleep disruption 10
stitch holders 17
stitch markers 17
stress fight or flight response 9, 10
stripy socks 36
Swiss darning see techniques,
  duplicate stitch

T
tape measure 15
techniques
  blocking 106–107
  cable stitch 79
  decreasing 103
  duplicate stitch 91
  Fair Isle 73
  increasing 102
  Kitchener stitch 39
  knitting in the round 31
  making a pompom 105
  mattress stitch 108–109
  picking up stitches 38
teddy bear 52
tension (gauge) 96
toy stuffing 17

U
unisex scarf 24

W
washcloths 22
wool needle 15

Y
yarn 14
  yarn weights
  1–3-ply (lace-weight) 14
  4-ply (fingering) 36, 41, 110
  aran (10-ply/worsted) 22, 44, 48, 58,
    66, 110
  chunky (bulky) 24
  DK (8-ply/light worsted) 30, 34, 52,
    62, 72, 78, 86, 90, 110
  super chunky (super bulky) 14, 26
  yarn type
  synthetic: acrylic, nylon, polyester,
    rayon, viscose 14
  natural yarns from animals: alpaca,
    angora, mohair, wool, cashmere 14
  natural yarns from plants: bamboo,
    cotton, hemp, linen 14
yarn bag 66

Acknowledgements

It's been such a pleasure to work with May Corfield, my editor at Search Press and Betsan Corkhill, founder of Stitchlinks. I've thoroughly enjoyed working as a team with these two inspirational ladies and have learned so many new things along the way.

I'm eternally grateful to Nancy from Woolgathering, for knitting up some beautiful samples when time was against me, and also to Fay for knitting up the neatest socks. I'd also like to thank DMC Creative World, Emily Foulds, Erika Knight, King Cole, Laughing Hens, Love Knitting, Rico, Rowan and Sublime for providing yarn support. I've used some of my favourite yarns in this book, all of which were a joy to knit with.

My thanks also to the wider team at Search Press, including their photographers, stylists and proofreaders, who always make my designs look amazing. And last but not least I'd like to thank you, the reader, for supporting my work and knitting up my designs.

Thank you all and happy knitting.

Lynne x